"Tim Riordan is more tha[...]
can relate to. From the [...]
nodding in agreement an[...]
doesn't just understand the struggle authors face when it
comes to marketing their books, he knows how to overcome
them. Offering action points and sound advice, *The Next
Bestseller* is by far the best book marketing book I have come
across."

> ~Heather Hart, Author of *Book Marketing 101*

"Tim Riordan provides solid book marketing advice with a
conversational style in his book, *The Next Bestseller: Marketing
for Success.*"

> ~Sarah Bolme, Author of *Your Guide to Marketing
> Christian Books*

"Great book if you or someone you care about has written
(or wants to write) and wants to sell their book. It's level-
headed, up-to-date, comprehensive and written in a manner
you can understand."

> ~Wayne Jenkins – Author of the *Ana Stilwell series;*
> Director of Missions, Western Baptist Association

"Tim Riordan addresses the real issues that make marketing
a book so difficult. The information he lays out throughout
the book is well organized and relevant to today's market-
place. I found this book to be a wealth of good information.
Authors would be wise to use it as a compass to get them
off the road of marketing frustration and onto the road of
marketing success."

> ~Scott Cahan for Readers' Favorite

"*The Next Best Seller- Book Marketing for Success* has hundreds of practical, cost-effective ideas for marketing your books. It covers every possible marketing strategy from email marketing, video marketing, public speaking, using Amazon to its fullest potential, and more. Following the strategies and tips he offers will help put your book on the bestseller list! I highly recommend this book!"

~Alexandria Bagnell – Author of *Abandoned into the Heart of God*

"For authors faced with a maze of book marketing options, *The Next Bestseller: Book Marketing for Success* is a great, comprehensive summary of the tricks of the trade. An impressive array of tips and strategies are explored here, and the book doesn't underdeliver. There's a lot of material packaged into The Next Bestseller that, if applied, can really take an author from beginner to polished, branded author over time."

~Sarah Scheele for Readers' Favorite

THE NEXT
BESTSELLER
BOOK MARKETING FOR SUCCESS

GreenTree Publishers

Newnan, GA

The Next Bestseller:
Book Marketing for Success

Printed in the United States of America
ISBN-13: 978-1-944483-33-3 (Greentree Publishers)

Follow Dr. Tim Riordan through these media links:
Website/blog: timriordan.com
Facebook: www.facebook.com/authortimriordan
Twitter: @tim_riordan

Greentree Publishers
www.greentreepublishers.com

Contents

Gift

We would like to share with you a helpful gift that will assist you in making your next book launch a wonderful success. We're simply calling it a "Book Launch Kit," and it's created by bestselling and award-winning author, Dr. Tim Riordan. In this kit, he offers information he has created to help your next launch be a success, including a book launch team job description, emails he has used to communicate with his launch team, a schedule of when to release launch resources, a list of helpful resources you can use to launch your book, and other useful tools. Receive your gift today by visiting the following site:

greentreepublishers.com/book-launch-kit.html.

Also, would you be willing to leave a review of this book on your retailer's website? Prospective readers will be helped and encouraged by your thoughtful comments.

We hope you enjoy your gift and find this book, *The Next Bestseller: Book Marketing for Success*, a helpful resource.

GreenTree Publishers

Chapter One

Do I Have to Market?

"You have got to be kidding!" We all know the feeling of being stunned by a bait and switch scheme. We thought we were going to a friend's house for dinner only to discover it was a vacuum cleaner demonstration. The one-hour presentation you had to sit through for the free vacation turned into a four-hour, twist-your-arm-until-you-said-uncle marathon that makes you think twice about "free vacations."

I felt this sense of disillusionment when I came to the place of getting my book published. I thought if you published your book through traditional means, the publisher did all of the marketing; after all, marketing and promotion are the two main reasons to go with traditional publishing. Right?

Wrong!

Brace yourself for the switch. Maybe publishers promoted every author's book in the past, and the authors only had to write, but those days are gone. If you desire to be a successful writer, you also have to be an intentional marketer, regardless of who publishes your book.

I met with a consultant while trying to decide which publishing direction I would go with my first nonfiction book, *Immovable: Standing Firm in the Last Days*. Though I had self-published my first novel, I wanted a "real publisher" to lead the charge with this book that contained the message about which I felt so passionately. The consultant informed me that whether self-published or traditionally published, I would still have most of the responsibility for the marketing. I waited for the punchline, but it never came. This revelation was no joke.

I signed up to be a writer, not a marketer. I had no interest in learning how to market. I did not get a degree in marketing, and it drives me crazy to see people pushing their books. I did not want to join the ranks of authors begging the world to *buy my book*. With no other choice, I was dragged kicking and screaming into the world of book marketing.

I accepted the fact if people were going to be impacted by the message of my books, *I* would have to market them. I also realized I had a lot to learn. I determined I would have to change my opinion and perspective about marketing. Fair warning, if you are to be a successful writer, you *must* be a successful marketer.

> *If you are going to be a successful writer, you must be a successful marketer.*

Time Well Spent

Accept that marketing is a necessary evil if you desire to spread your message. Okay, so marketing is not evil, but it felt that way to me at first. I still do not enjoy taking the time needed to market my books, but I accept it as essential. I had to change my perspective and see myself as not pushing my books but as proclaiming my message. I am not only sharing my message, but also building relationships.

If I believe people need to read *Immovable* so they will be prepared to stand firm in the days ahead, I need to figure out a way to let people know my book exists. If I want readers to be impacted by life-altering lessons in the book of

Proverbs, I need to tell potential readers about my book, *Wisdom Speaks: Life Lessons from Proverbs*. I'm not pushing my product to finance a new car, though there's nothing wrong with making a profit from writing. I'm inviting people to be changed by reading the message I feel compelled to share.

In today's age of social media, I am developing relationships with readers so my writing will be the words of a trusted friend. As writers, our objective is life change in readers. Our mission is so critical that we must be willing to do what it takes to make sure our message gets out to the world. This commitment calls us to think how best to market our messages.

The Business of Writing

In addition to thinking like a writer, we must also think of ourselves as entrepreneurs or business owners. An entrepreneur has to be creative and willing to be a risk taker, and our business is promoting the message about which we felt so strongly that we put it in a book. As writers, we have to look for ways to connect with potential readers, and at times, that connection does involve risk. It may be the risk of spending fifty dollars on an advertising promotion, or it may be a greater financial investment. It may be the risk of trying something new or venturing into new territory that everyone but God tells you is not a good idea.

As business owners, we have to be careful with the details of our businesses. I may cover this topic in another book, but we must be committed to keeping up with our expenses and planning our marketing budget. Like a business owner who does not keep up with his finances will fail, we also will fail if we do not take a proper approach to this aspect of writing. Laying a proper business foundation takes time, but in the long run, our diligence will prove successful.

I also had to accept that I needed financial capital to do further promotion of my books, so making a profit is not a bad thing. Just as it's okay for me to accept a salary from my church, it's okay for me to make a profit from writing. With hard work, it's possible to make a good profit from writing. I urge you not to enlarge your retirement plans yet because most writers do not make a lot of money through writing and publishing. Some do, but most make enough to recoup expenses and maybe have enough left to take their families to Disney World. Some self-publishers have done well financially, but I choose not to make that my sole objective.

I include the way we think about financing in this section because, at times, I feel guilty charging for my books. If I had my way, I would give them away. The problem with this approach is I cannot afford to give everyone copies of my books. I do not have the financial capital needed to promote my books unless I earn extra income from sales. While publishers may create a small budget for marketing (and I emphasize the word *small* for authors who have yet to make the bestseller list), as a self-publisher, you probably have *no* budget for marketing. My marketing plan includes a lot of free ideas, but sometimes you incur expenses. I remind myself often if I do not charge for my books, there is someone in the world who will never have the opportunity to be impacted by my message. It takes money to market my book to someone living in Chicago or the U.K., so making a profit is essential.

While I have established that it is possible to make a profit from publishing your book, you should review your real purpose for writing. Do you want to make a living by writing and publishing? There is nothing wrong with this goal, but I have a feeling that your goal goes much deeper than improving your cash flow. Why are you writing? Answering

> *Understanding the "Why" of your writing gives you greater clarity on the "What" and the "How."*

this question will provide a guiding star that not only affects what you write but also impacts how you market your book once it's complete.

I want people to experience life change through the liberating message of God's truth. This goal ignites my energies daily as I consider ways to get my message out to as many people as possible. Because I want life change in my readers, I must *have* readers. Holding a book in my hand with my name on the cover was never my objective. Life change in people's lives compels me to spend time every day marketing my books.

How does your goal ignite your energy to write and market? You may not be a pastor, or you may write novels instead of nonfiction books. The genre doesn't matter. You have a reason for writing. You want to create something in the lives of readers, even if it's simply encouragement or entertainment. Your mission will inspire your marketing.

It's the Small Things that Matter

In a previous book, I issued the challenge to write every day. Now I am adding an additional challenge: **market every day**. I know that time constraints are a real challenge, but again, I urge you to follow the principle of small steps. I mentioned in another book that early on I committed myself to writing for an hour a day. I now have to include marketing in that hour on many days because my time is limited. I sometimes schedule an extended period on a day off to review or rewrite my marketing plan.

I encourage you not to reject the notion that you can market your books. Your message is too valuable not to give your best effort. You may even want to hire someone to help you with marketing if you don't have time to do it yourself. You might be amazed at what a little marketing will accomplish. Last week, *Songs from the Heart* moved into the #1 spot on the best sellers list on Amazon, and this week, *The Long Way Home* became a #1 bestseller again. You can be an effective marketer too.

You will have to make decisions about how to spend your time, but if you are determined, you can find time to be a writer and a marketer. We must quit thinking we don't have time to be writers. We have the same amount of time as anyone else; it is a matter of how we choose to use it. I manage my time for writing by not watching television. I may watch the news from time to time, and sometimes the lure of college football draws me. I have decided, however, watching television excessively is not good for me anyway, and it doesn't help me accomplish my life goals. You have to plan time in your schedule every week to work your marketing plan. Remember it is the small steps taken consistently that bring about great strides.

One of my sons is a Christian song writer, recording artist, and producer. A few years ago, he and his band (Atlas Rhoads) released an album that he recorded in his studio. I suppose self-producing is quite similar to self-publishing. He frequents a site on Facebook where people discuss sound equipment and items related to guitars. He posted a link on that site for his new album. A major producer from Nashville saw the link, listened to Timothy's work, and watched the music video to one of his songs, *Bride*. Four days after the initial self-release of the album, this producer contacted the top three record labels in Nashville and told them to sign my son's band.

Since then, Timothy has talked with two companies, done additional work in Nashville as a writer, is a featured soloist on one of Word Records worship albums, and had the opportunity to join other popular Christian bands for cross-country and international tours. While God was directing events for my son, it was the little thing of posting an announcement on a Facebook page that helped open the door for him to have an international stage for his ministry.

We may also need to change the way we think about people buying our books. If our goal is to make money, then a potential book buyer is simply a means to an end, which is our financial gain. If our goal is to generate change in the lives of our readers, we realize our readers are *the end*. If we do not understand this distinction, we think our connection with readers is over as soon as they purchase our books. When the goal is life change in our readers, this perspective changes our motives and reactions to social media, speaking engagements, and book signings.

Building relationships with readers brings about great dividends in their lives. When people and life change are the objectives, we talk with people at the book table and respond to their Facebook posts with genuine concern and interest.

I have a feeling no one reading this book would say they signed up to be a marketer. You just want to write, and you want people to read your books. If your message is worth reading, then it's worth promoting. I offer important marketing guidelines in the following pages that will help anyone become a successful marketer. Success requires serious work and consistent planning.

I once had an insurance salesman tell me that no one plans to fail; they just fail to plan. That statement is trite, but it's true. What does a marketing plan look like? We will look at several aspects of this concept, but the key is to have a plan. The next chapter focuses on a few important principles that could make the difference between you being a best-seller or a writer no one has ever heard of, much less read.

Action Points
- What is your reaction to marketing your book? Make a list of the top five reasons you should improve your marketing skills.
- How might thinking of yourself as a business owner improve your writing success? What do you anticipate being your greatest struggles in dealing with the business end of writing? What are some steps you can take to turn these weaknesses into strengths?

- Writing and marketing take time. Because you only have twenty-four hours in a day, you may have to stop doing something to create more opportunity for writing. Evaluate your time and decide what you will give up to accomplish your goals. Share your commitment with your spouse or close friend.

- Do you need to change the way you think about making money through writing or about selling your books to readers? Make a list of five reasons why you need to make a profit in your writing. Write out a brief financial plan indicating how you will use the income from your books.

Chapter Two

Planning to Plan

I'm sure you remember the famous line from *Field of Dreams*, "If you build it, they will come." I must have gone into writing believing the author's version of that movie's theme: "If I write it, they will read." That idea worked on a Hollywood, make-believe farm in Iowa, but it will not work in the world of writing. Your book may rival *War and Peace* or *The Purpose-Driven Life*, but if no one knows it exists, it will become a doorstop for your basement door or kindling for a bonfire this fall.

Marketing is essential for book sales. Whether you self-publish or go with a traditional publisher, marketing becomes *your* responsibility. While doorstops are useful and bonfires can be fun, the message in our books is too important for such benign tasks. The challenge is to figure out how to market and when to start. This book will address the "how to" of marketing, but when is the best time to begin marketing? Because I never considered having to market my books, I never thought about when to market them. In short, the time to market is now.

Ready, Set, Go!

You can never put your plan into action too soon. An author's platform takes a while to develop, so you should lay the groundwork for your platform *before* your book is written. If you have already written your book but don't have a marketing plan, do not feel you have made a huge mistake.

It only means you are a little behind but catching up is possible. Think of Dave Wottle in the 1972 Olympics. He won the gold medal in the 800-meter final after dropping to the rear of the pack for the first 500 meters. He passed every competitor to beat the favored runner by .03 of a second, earning the nickname "Wottle the Throttle."

Working on a marketing strategy *before* writing not only helps you promote your books but also helps you understand your readers. Understanding your readers *before* you write will help you write more effectively for those you are going to reach.

Another advantage of marketing first is it gives you more time to build your platform. Though I address platform building in another chapter, know the bigger the platform, the greater the impact. I'm writing with the assumption most people reading this book will not have a large platform. Having a small platform at the beginning of your writing career does not hinder your book from being a success, but you will need to work harder to reach more people.

> "A platform is the thing you have to stand on to get heard."
>
> Michael Hyatt

Social media has engulfed our culture, and you can build a large platform, regardless of your circumstances. Building a platform, however, takes time, so begin this process now. I will do my best to guide you, but I recommend you read other resources and speak with others who have been successful. This book will cover different ideas and serve as an introduction. You may need additional study on various topics to become proficient.

Marketing before you write gives you the opportunity to involve potential readers in the writing process. Remember we live in a time of instant accessibility. Authors no longer write from atop their ivory towers. Building relationships with readers is important if you're going to have a broader reach. As you begin the marketing journey, invite readers to participate. By doing so, you'll build anticipation of your publication. I did this with my book on Psalms, *Songs from the Heart,* by inviting people on Facebook to tell me about their favorite Psalm and why it was their favorite. I also had them vote on two options for a cover design.

You can create reader interest by taking surveys or inviting dialogue. Many authors blog about their topic and invite readers to interact on the subject. Anything you do to get people to respond will be a plus when you release your book. I suggest you create a way to sign up for an email newsletter or some type of correspondence you can send out periodically to keep them updated (see Chapter Thirteen). Regardless of what you do to build your platform, remember we live in the age of internet relationships.

Focused Energy

As you begin marketing, it's easy to get overwhelmed by the immensity of the challenge. You may feel like quitting at times because the task seems daunting. I urge you to consider the power of focused energy. At first, I was overwhelmed with marketing because I kept hearing of all the things I had to do to be a success. Although a few critical steps are essential if you are to be a successful writer, you do not have to employ every marketing tactic known to humanity. I tend to hear about a strategy someone is using and feel I must start using it. I encourage you to remember this principle: *focused energy has more impact than scattered effort.*

I can turn on my flashlight and illuminate a dark place with a beam of light. If I focus that light into a laser beam, I can cut through metal. Focused light has greater strength than diffused light. When I describe all of the social media outlets, do not feel you must use them all at first. Start with one or two and give them focused energy. In another chapter, I write about the marketing web. Choose a few steps I will recommend and give them your best effort. I believe you will find focused energy brings much greater results than scattered effort.

Build upon marketing success over time. Find something that works and pour yourself into it. Experiment with other options and study different methods before discarding them; however, do not be discouraged if you are not tweeting, posting, blogging, snap chatting, and instagramming (I think I made that word up) every hour.

> "If you go to work on your goals, your goals will go to work on you."
>
> Jack Canfield

In this book, you'll see I present a process that grows out of the principle of first things. You'll start with a basic platform and build upon it as you have opportunity.

The Power of Daily

Do not underestimate the power of doing something every day. The subtitle to one of John Maxwell's books states, "The secret of your success is determined by your daily agenda."[1] You cannot lose weight in a day. Losing weight requires us to change habits and start new disciplines we do every day. Writing and marketing success follow the same principle.

One of American author Earl Nightingale's famous quotes underscores the important principle of developing the daily discipline of focused study:

> One hour per day of study in your chosen field is all it takes. One hour per day of study will put you at the top of your field within three years. Within five years you'll be a national authority. In seven years, you can be one of the best people in the world at what you do.[2]

Although I'm focusing on writing and marketing, I think Nightingale's principle applies. If we give attention to the art of writing and the practice of marketing for one hour per day, we will see great dividends.

I'm sure the return would be much greater if we could spend one hour per day writing *and* one hour per day marketing, but we are busy people. It's possible you're already working fifty to sixty hours per week. Finding an hour per day may be a challenge, but it can be done.

In one of my earlier books, I shared I became a published author when I developed the discipline of writing one hour per day. I usually found this hour during lunch, excluding Sundays. Lunch meetings with other people hindered me from my goal sometimes. Because my schedule is as crazy as yours, there were days I wasn't able to write at all. In general, though, I did my best to devote an hour a day to the task, five or six days a week. After a few years, I published my first book.

During the writing phase of my first book, part of my "one hour a day" discipline included marketing my book to publishers and learning how to self-publish. Once I began writing more books, my daily discipline included learning how to market. Although I try to market a little *every* day, I have altered my schedule to write every day and focus on marketing three days a week. With small changes in my daily schedule, I have become a published author of multiple books. You can experience the same success with intentional focus on writing and marketing.

Just Do It

As you consider the prospects of becoming a marketer, you may decide you would rather go back to Greek class and parse some verbs or try to explain the theory of relativity to a preschooler. Trust me, marketing is not that bad. Employ the age-old axiom: Don't just sit there; do something.

In the foreword to *Build Your Author Platform* by Carole Jelen and Michael McCallister, Jack Canfield (co-author of the *Chicken Soup for the Soul* series) said he practices the *Rule of Five*.[3] The *Rule of Five* means Canfield executes at least five things a day to market his book. He may contact five bloggers in an effort to have a guest blog published or send out five free copies of his book to movers and shakers in the world. He challenges readers to be creative and simply pledge themselves to doing at least five things a day to get their books out there so readers will know it exists. I think we all agree that evidently Canfield and company did something right. The *Rule of Five* may be his secret weapon that is no longer secret.

Take the Plunge

We have determined your message is important enough that you were willing to spend months putting it down on paper. This commitment says your message is worth making marketing sacrifices so readers will purchase your book. There is a learning curve, and I will do my best to make the journey as easy as possible.

Hundreds, even thousands, of people are waiting to be impacted by the message of your book. They just do not know it exists yet. Turn to the next chapter and start the journey that could one day lead Jack Canfield to give you a call for marketing advice.

Action Points

- Have you ever felt like you could not be a successful author because you do not have a large platform? Are you willing to set aside your preconceived opinions about the task of becoming an author and put together a plan to help you reach the masses?
- It's never too early to start marketing. What are three things you can do now to market your future book?
- As you write your book, how can you involve future readers? Make a brief list of a few things you will do through social media to begin building interest now.

- In this chapter, I emphasized the importance of focused energy. Write down three things you can do to focus your energy on marketing.

- Do you agree with Earl Nightingale that you could become an expert at anything just through studying one hour per day? What are you willing to do daily so you can be a successful writer? Are you willing to learn marketing tips to help you succeed as an author, and are you willing to do them daily?

- How can you implement the *Rule of Five* today? Think of five things you can do today to promote your book.

Chapter Three

Enlarging Your Platform

Several years ago, I began the laborious process of trying to secure an agent and a publisher. After a number of rejections, I received a letter from an agent saying he liked my book and would represent me if I enlarged my platform. Though I had an idea about the concept of platform, I didn't have a clue how to make it bigger. From my limited, pastor's perspective, a platform is established by the size of my church or my role in denominational life. Church size and denominational involvement helps, but I have learned platform building involves much more.

The bottom line is publishers are looking for people who have visibility with readers. Before they sign a contract with you, they want to know you can reach a target audience. They want to know you are connected to enough potential readers to get a return on their investment. Because publishers must consider the financial bottom line of all contracts, their concerns are legitimate.

Even as a self-published author, finances play an important role. Although authors' main goal is to expand their readership so their message has greater impact, income will influence the marketing budget of a self-published author. A growing number of self-published authors are becoming full-time writers and depend upon their writing income for day-to-day expenses.

The concept of platform building is not just for authors who are traditionally published. It is for any writer who wants to influence people through their books.

What Is Platform?

You will often read about the importance of a platform, but what does that mean? You could compare it to a foundation of a house. Years ago, when Sandra and I moved our family to a new ministry field, we began the arduous task of shopping for a house. We found some land we liked, and someone had already constructed a foundation for a home on it. The only problem was the house that would fit the foundation would not fit our family's needs. The size of a foundation determines the size of the house.

> *"Your platform encompasses how you can reach an audience of customers right now, or how you plan to do so in the future."*
>
> Joanna Penn

The size of your platform will determine the size of your influence through writing. I want to be careful and not say that you will be able to influence only the number of people who have chosen to "like" your author page on Facebook or sign up for your email newsletter, but I think you can see the importance of a base from which you connect with people. Unusual circumstances could expand your writing career, and thankfully, God is not limited to your followers on Twitter. In general, however, if you want to reach more people with your written message, build a larger platform.

Courtney Carpenter from *Writer's Digest* stated, "Platform, simply put, is your *visibility as an author*."[1] Publishers view your platform as your ability to sell books through your networks, relationships, opportunities, and social media outlets. We can see our platform as the base from which we influence others.

Author and writing coach Jane Friedman included four key components that should be in our platforms: visibility, authority, proven reach, and target audience.[2] Who really knows you, and what credibility will you have with readers? Do you have a measurable impact on a sizable audience? These are significant questions as you consider the importance of expanding your influence.

> *"You have to believe, in the deepest part of your soul, that it is a good thing for readers to buy and read your book."*
>
> Tim Grahl

I once had an agent tell me to increase my Twitter followers to 2,000 and then get back in touch with him. Though I'm sure he doesn't limit platform to just Twitter followers, he seemed to be putting a lot of eggs in that social media basket. We tend to define platform by our influence on social media, but it is much more.

Brooke Warner, an author and writing coach (see warner coaching.com), suggested several key elements that should be included in a platform of a nonfiction writer and offered a breakdown by percentage (see graph below).[3] Fiction writers can find a similar application of these percentages.

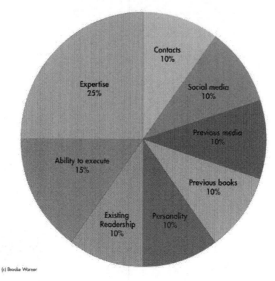

This book will focus on a number of tools or steps that will help you build a solid platform. In this chapter, I will share basic ideas you must consider as you begin the task of expanding your reach as an author. The following chapters focus on the nuts and bolts of creating a sufficient platform so your books end up in the hands of a lot of readers.

Remember Your Purpose

I have been a pastor for almost forty years, and during my ministry, I have experienced "the good, the bad, and the ugly" of ministry life. Most of us have probably written a letter of resignation a number of times only to throw it into the trashcan. During those difficult days, I have found that I have to often go back to my calling. I do not serve in ministry because of a paycheck or because of the thrill of having crowds of people come to hear me speak each week. I do not do what I do for the affirmation or acceptance by the people in my congregation. I am a pastor because God has called me to serve.

As we work to build our author platform, we must often remind ourselves of our calling. For me as a Christian, my real purpose is to influence people to grow in their relationship with Jesus Christ. Your passion may be to educate people about good health or guide people to financial independence. Whatever your purpose, I hope you can think of it in terms of helping others and connect your purpose for writing your book to your personal calling.

> *"Defining your message is essentially writing out your vision with your ideal readers in mind. A lot of marketers will call this your promise — it's what you are promising your readers they will get by reading your book."*
>
> Heather Hart

I was reviewing my book sales a while back and noted that my first nonfiction book, *Immovable: Standing Firm in the Last Days*, was not selling as many copies as it had when first published. Many times, the novels I write under a pen name sell much better. I was a little discouraged and thought about how I could improve my sales.

I went to a meeting made up of representatives from a number of churches in my city, and I arrived a little late because of a previous commitment. I entered as unobtrusively as possible and sat in the back. At the conclusion of the meeting, a gentleman stood to make an announcement. He said he had read a book by Tim Riordan called *Immovable:*

*Standing Firm in the Last D*ays and felt burdened about doing something to help other believers prepare for the days ahead. He has started a prayer and discipleship group in the community and now has a number of people in attendance. He invited people to consider either joining his group or starting their own groups.

I do not think the man even knows who I am, and I don't believe he knew I happened to be in the building. Needless to say, my fire was lit when I realized that my book *was* having an impact. While my numbers over the last couple of weeks are not what I want them to be, God is accomplishing His purpose through me and my book to advance His Kingdom. My ultimate mission is not just to sell books but rather to encourage life change.

As you work on building your platform, keep the "why you write" at the forefront of your mind. This reminder will affect what you do and how you do it. It will keep you centered and well grounded. You will be reminded your writing career is not about you and your goals. It is about accomplishing your purpose. You will want to "keep score" by evaluating your sales, but the real win will come as you accomplish your purpose. We don't want to excuse poor marketing by hoping someone will be changed by the sale of only a few of our books, but at the same time, lives can be changed one book at a time.

Enlarge Your Network

I tend to cringe when I hear someone name dropping or when I happen to meet someone who seems more intent on who I know rather than in getting to know me. Enlarging our network of relationships with other people, however, is an important part of spreading our message. Networking can be a challenge for some authors because we are often, by nature, more introverted than outgoing. I have not done a study on the personalities of authors, but I know that an author must spend many hours in research and writing, which adds up to a lot of alone time.

If you are an introvert, you may be the kind of person who carries a book with you to social events or at least finds a corner away from the crowd where you can review your week's priorities while everyone else mingles. Those illustrations may be a bit of an exaggeration, but I know I prefer to be alone instead of in a crowd. This reality means networking with other people is not in the center of my comfort zone. You may think that statement odd coming from a person who speaks to hundreds of people every Sunday morning, but it's true. I don't think I am socially challenged, and frankly I couldn't

> "The currency of networking is not greed but generosity."
>
> Keith Ferrazzi

be a pastor if I didn't possess the ability to interact with people on a regular basis. It's kind of hard to shepherd the flock if you don't want to be around the flock. I want to be around the flock, but I also enjoy being alone. I do, however, find a lot of my strengths in ministry are expressed during times of personal study, prayer, and writing.

If you lean toward being more of an introvert than the life of the party, you may find networking doesn't come naturally to you. Just because something doesn't come naturally doesn't mean you should avoid it. I dare say you do many things in your life you do not enjoy or that would not be considered a strength. I do my taxes every year even though I'm not good at it, and I hate it. I file my tax return because it must be done. Hopefully, networking with others will not fall into the painful category of filing a form 1040 with the IRS, but you may find being intentional in your desire to reach out to other people requires a bit of discipline.

> "Nothing can expand your marketing reach quite like several influencers promoting your book. Influencers are people who will get other people…to buy your book."
>
> Tim Grahl

Networking is an important part of our writing aspirations. If you're a Christian, it's a key part of the Christian life. God made us to exist in community. I usually find if I make myself attend a social event when I'd rather stay alone in my study, I leave the event glad I made the effort. It's like eating steamed vegetables instead of fried food. We may enjoy the fried food at first, but the steamed vegetables eventually make us feel so much better. God hard-wired into every human being the need for meaningful relationships with other people. Our lives will flourish in proportion to the way we connect with others.

I must mention a caution about networking. We need to be careful never to look at a person as a means to another person. Our lives, and writing careers, or ministries are about relationships, and every person matters. The day we lead a person to feel like they are only a tool to help us connect with someone "more important" is the day our influence potential will begin moving down a slippery slope toward ultimate ineffectiveness. People know when we genuinely care about them, and they know when we view them as pawns to a greater cause.

I attended the Southern Baptist Convention meeting and ran into a former classmate. The whole time we talked, my "friend" was waving to people passing by who pastored larger churches or had important roles in Convention life. I ended my conversation with him in the middle of a sentence, and he didn't even realize it. While networking with people does help us connect with others, the first person in the chain is just as important as the last person.

The Power of Proximity

Networking is an important path to connecting our message to the masses. In 1929, Frigyes Karinthy wrote a short story entitled *Chains* that presents the principle of "Six Degrees of Separation." *Science Alert* author Fiona MacDonald explained the principle, "The idea is that anyone on the planet can be connected to anyone else in just six steps. So through just five other people, you're effectively connected to the Queen of England, Tom Cruise, or even a Mongolian sheep herder."[4] I do not know whether I actually have just six steps to anyone in the world, but the concept leads me to understand I'm a lot closer to the Queen of England or the president of the United States than I may have imagined. Through connecting to other people via social media or Chamber of Commerce meet and greets, we may find the person who can help turn our book into a bestseller.

How do we enlarge our network? In the old days, enlarging our network meant sharing more business cards at social gatherings. While business cards can still play a part in networking, other methods continue to surface that will help us expand our reach. Whether or not we love social media, we must admit that it is here to stay. If we want to grow our influence, social media will be an important part of our strategy. We can expand our network by gaining more followers on Twitter, increasing our friend-base on Facebook, or securing more LinkedIn connections.

> *"You can have everything in life you want if you will just help enough other people get what they want."*
>
> Zig Ziggler

We can also increase our network by attending social events or training workshops. Securing speaking engagements will put us into places where we can meet more people. Sometimes meeting others will take place in virtual environments, such as Amazon book reviews, blogs, or interactions on Goodreads. As you read the remaining chapters in this book, you will discover many ways you can connect to other people. I suggest you begin a list of ways you plan to meet more people in order to broaden your writing platform.

Building a strong platform is such an important principle for becoming a successful author. You cannot overestimate its importance. Before leaving the topic, I want to share a few practical suggestions in the next chapter you can consider as you develop a plan to strengthen your base and reach more people with your message.

Action Points

- How would you describe the size of your author's platform? What does it include?
- Does the size of your platform, as it is today, discourage you from writing? Make a list of three to five reasons why enlarging your platform is important for you.
- Look over Brooke Warner's graph that presents several key elements of an author's platform. On a scale of 1 - 10 (with 1 being not very effective and 10 being excellent), rate yourself on each element.
- Have you taken the time to write out a purpose statement for your writing ministry or career? If not, begin that process now.
- Are you an introvert or an extrovert? What will you have to do to improve your networking skills and enlarge your author platform based upon your personality?
- Do you agree with Frigyes Karinthy's opinion about *Six Degrees of Separation*? Does his belief inspire you to do everything in your power to market your books because you are only six people away from influencing anyone in the world?

Chapter Four

Your Platform's Foundation

Does a foundation have a foundation? Sort of. If I were writing a book on pouring a concrete slab for your house, I could write about different ingredients for your concrete or different ratios of sand, cement, and rock. We could also consider the role of concrete footers under your slab. I guess a foundation can have a foundation. How does this apply to expanding our writer's platform? Much of this book will deal with specifics on how to enlarge our platforms, but we must take a moment to consider the basics of a strong platform.

It's a Dialogue

Building a platform as an author is about developing relationships. I am a Christian, so the first relationship I want to develop is with my heavenly Father. If you are a Christian writer, I assume you pray about everything. I pray about my marketing strategy. Why not? Sometimes, I don't have a clue what I'm doing, but God knows all things. God will always guide us to the best practice and strategy.

Writing and marketing also involves growing relationships with other people. Everything we do as a writer relates to people. Our objective is not just to write a book, and our mission is not just to make money. We write to engage people with a life-altering message. Tim Grahl's comment in *Your First 1000 Copies* underscores the importance of relationships well, "Marketing is two things: (1) creating lasting connections with people through (2) a focus on being relentlessly helpful."[1]

Since enlarging our platforms is an extension of our mission, our platforms have more to do with engaging people than selling a product. I know many of the ideas I share in this book could fit into the sterile topic of marketing and sales, but the bottom line must always be people not quotas. The end product of our mission is changed lives and not increased sales. Understanding this aspect of marketing, we must see the act of marketing our books as a dialogue and not a monologue.

If marketing were a monologue, we could see it as standing on a street corner with a megaphone shouting, "Buy my book!" As a dialogue, we engage people in conversations that lead to life change. I don't think any of us would disagree that our lives, ministries, or careers are about people. Dialogue plays a central role as we build relationships with others. We err, however, when we think relationship building doesn't start until marketing efforts have ended.

> "Customers don't want ads, they want conversations."
>
> Brandon Evans

People are not interested in being a number in your sales report. They would rather be a person who is considered and understood. If we are going to be successful marketers, we must think how to engage people through a marketing strategy. We may or may not talk to a person face-to-face as a result of the marketing process. Yet our interactions with people through advertising, back cover material, or social media should always be about the needs of the customer and not about selling another book. Keeping this thought in mind helps us develop a marketing strategy that touches people's hearts instead of reaching for their wallets.

Plan to Succeed

Failure is not an option. This realization became the motivational theme behind NASA's push to the moon during the 1960s. President Kennedy said during his inauguration speech in 1961 the United States would have a man on the moon before the end of the decade. During a tour of the space center in Florida, I was reminded when Kennedy made that famous declaration, the technology did not exist to accomplish that mission.

I am sure putting a man on the moon was important and brought about essential results, but NASA's mission pales in comparison to helping people become all God means them to be. Life was never intended to be a solo act. We all find fulfillment in giving, serving, and helping others. As writers, we have a divine opportunity to connect people to God's greater life purpose. The world is counting on us, so we must not fail in our mission.

My mother passed away in 2016. Much of who I am today, at least the good part, came about because of her consistent shaping of my life as a young boy. She told me throughout my earlier life, "You can do anything you want to do if you want to do it badly enough." She taught me I couldn't fail as long as I planned to succeed. It is because of her encouragement I grew up thinking I could do anything I wanted to do. I would just have to figure out how to do it. I used to say to myself if someone else could do something, so could I. This belief is a little flawed, but it has led me to attempt many things and succeed at some of them.

If you want to be a writer, you can be one. If you want to be a good writer and are willing to pay the price, you can be a good writer. I assume you are reading this book because

> "If you can dream it, you can do it."
> Enzo Ferrari

you are a writer, and now, you want to do a better job at marketing. I hope you will not strive just to publish books; instead, I hope you will work hard to publish books that change lives.

If someone else can become a bestselling author, so can you. If Jack Canfield can write a book that touches the hearts of millions of readers, your book can also have a broad reach and a global impact. You need to figure out how to make it happen. Your commitment to succeed plus persistence and creativity, multiplied by God working through your efforts, will bring about significant mission success. Failure is not an option, so figure out how you will navigate to success.

Above All Things, Be Ethical

I would like to think I do not need to include a section about integrity. I know, however, how easy it is to be pulled in directions by ungodly motivations. Sometimes those motivations that lead to unethical behavior may not be bad motivations. For example, wanting our book to be a best seller is not a bad goal, and if it motivates us to work hard at marketing our book, best seller aspirations can be healthy. If we choose unethical behavior, however, that healthy goal

just became a motivation to move us down a path away from
God.

You may have read about business leaders, politicians,
or pastors who started out with pure motives and wholesome goals only to be pulled down
by unethical actions. I think we are
mature enough to know any of us
could fall into similar traps. We
must create guidelines and strategies that will keep us on the
straight and narrow and hold us

> *"Relativity applies
> to physics, not
> ethics."*
> **Albert Einstein**

accountable. It would also be a good idea to have close
friends hold us accountable to our writing goals as well.
Nothing is more motivating than to have a solid friend periodically ask us *tough questions* about our writing. Accountability will help us check egos at the door and wash impure
motives down the drain.

In the area of marketing, it could be easy to fall into
strategies that are shady. For example, you could pay someone to write a review for you and probably no one would
know the difference. You could reason with yourself that
other review services, such as Kirkus or Readers' Favorite,
charge, so why should the good people at Amazon care if
you slipped a paid review in your list of customer reviews?

Amazon has a strict policy about this practice. If someone is caught trying to buy reviews, their book could be re-
moved from the Amazon platform. I will address the
challenge of getting reviews in another chapter that will
hopefully help you get more in the best ways, though this is
a battle I struggle with, too. You may also find one shady

7">

move leads you to do something that's not just shady but dark.

I am motivated by the words of Colossians 3:17, "Whatever you do in word or deed, do all in the name of the Lord Jesus." Doing something in the name of Jesus means whatever I am doing should be done with the character of Christ or reflecting the name of Jesus to the world.

How will this principle be lived out in your marketing efforts? I do not know every way we might be tempted, but I'm sure God will tap you on the shoulder when you turn left instead of right. You may be tempted to pay for followers, exaggerate book sales, or be dishonest about a personal story; however, we'll find the high road is always the best road. Inflating your book sales may get you special status and recognition, but your house of cards could fall down around you. I know of one pastor who was fired partly because of unethical behavior related to book sales. Doing the right thing is always the right thing.

Run Like a Turtle

It might appear that some authors become overnight successes, but in most cases, no one is an overnight success. It is the consistent, steady pace of a marathon runner that wins the race. I ran cross country part of the time I was in college. We were warned about the "jack rabbits" on the other teams. These guys were usually the slowest runners on the team and would be put out front to draw out the best runners from the opponent. The jack rabbit would take off at a fast pace and try to tire out the competition so the other runners on his team could win the race.

Most successful writers and marketers are turtles and not rabbits. Slow and steady is a good motto. As you read through this book, you will begin developing strategies for marketing. Plan your work and work your plan. When you're done, do it again. Stay the course. Evaluate your plan. Then plan some more. You will find your persistent efforts will pay off.

Action Points

- Do you pray about your writing? Have you ever considered praying about marketing?
- In this chapter, I said our platform has more to do with engaging people than selling a product. How do you engage people through marketing? Can you list three ways engaging people could be possible?
- Think about the difference between a dialogue and a monologue. Write down a few ways marketing could just be a monologue and how to change it into a dialogue.
- Sometimes, it is easy to fail before we begin. What is your reaction to the *failure is not an option* section? What practices should you develop that will ensure success in writing and marketing?
- Will you make a pledge to be ethical? Do you have an accountability partner? If not, will you find one? Come up with a list of questions relating to your writing that you would like your friend to ask you from time to time.
- Are you in the writing business for the long haul? Your success may be slow at first. What things could you do to stay focused when it seems you are not succeeding?

Chapter Five

Defining Your Brand

If you happened to be riding through central Mexico on horseback in the late 16th century, you may have come across cattle with three crosses burned on their hides. If you didn't know any better, you'd think someone was creating a new method for evangelism. After looking into it, you discover that Hernan Cortes burned the crosses in his cattle so everyone would know they belonged to him. Cortes brought branding to the new world, but today it has found a whole new expression.

For the last 400 years, branding has been used to signify identity. Although cattle were some of the first victims of the branding iron, today the topic of branding is so specialized that many companies employ experts to help establish their brand. We no longer use hot irons as much as symbols, slogans, and jingles, but branding is here to stay. What does branding have to do with writing and marketing? A lot!

Author and writing coach Nina Amir believes it's essential for authors to develop their brand. She said, "Serious writers who want to succeed as authors should include branding in their early success planning."[1] That is quite a statement. I cannot imagine any writer saying they do not want to succeed. According to Amir, creating a brand is paramount to a writer's success.

You may have had a similar thought as I when I first considered the concept of branding: I understood the need for a company like Nike or Google to create a recognizable brand, but did I really need a brand attached to my name or my books? You may be surprised by the answer.

What is an Author Brand?

Branding points to a method as well as an identity. We can see it as both a noun and a verb. Companies introduce themselves to potential customers through a brand. It's easy to consider the Nike swoosh or the Coca-Cola waves as an important part of branding, but how does branding apply to you? What is your identity?

We might think of the purpose of a brand as a means to imprint a product into the minds of potential customers. While being memorable is part of the purpose, a brand has a much greater objective. Whether we are talking about selling shoes or books, the purpose of a brand is similar. Author Kimberly Grabas helps us to understand the meaning of an author's brand: "Simply put, your brand is your promise to your audience…It tells them what they can expect from you and your work, and it differentiates what you have to offer from that of your competitors."[2]

I am expecting a pair of NB's to arrive in the mail today. Do those two letters communicate what will be in my package? What if I put some white slash marks that are pointed on one end through the "N"? You probably guessed that I'm getting New Balance shoes today. While the logo, which could just be the N on the side of the shoe or the NB on the box, tells me what's in the box, the brand is more than just a title or logo. I wear New Balance shoes because I have found them to be the best shoes for my feet. I've been wearing the same type of shoe for years because they promise quality and deliver it. When I purchase a pair of New Balance shoes, I know what to expect.

Your brand will introduce yourself to your potential audience and endear you to your readers. Whether you write books for the family (James Dobson), for leadership development (John Maxwell), or another topic that touches the lives of people, your audience will know what to expect when they see your name on the cover. Although your brand could include a logo or a color scheme, it falls more in line with a concept, theme, and quality. If you read a book by John Maxwell, you know he's going to give you a book filled with practical guidelines about how to be a better leader.

Why Do Authors Need a Brand?

A strong brand for authors means more readers. When people latch onto your brand, they sort of become a part of your family. Seth Godin calls this family a tribe.[3] In the past, we might try to mass market our message to everyone. It was the shotgun approach to marketing, but Godin says marketing today has become more streamlined. Instead of trying to convince people to buy our books, we find people who need to read our messages and introduce them to the resource they've been looking for—our book. Godin says your potential readers are a "group that is disconnected but already has a yearning." How we present ourselves, our brands, will determine who decides to join our tribes.

Not much thought is required to realize that as our tribes increase, our book sales increase and our influence has the opportunity to bear more fruit in people's lives. If we work hard on the front end of marketing to determine the best way to present ourselves, we'll have greater success at growing large tribes of book-hungry readers.

A strong brand will also lead to blind sales. I usually read the back cover of a book, book reviews, and the table of contents before I make a purchase. Recently, I purchased a book by seeing only the title and author. The reason I made the purchase was because of the author's brand. I am a part of John Ortberg's tribe, so when I saw that he had a book entitled *Love Beyond Reason* and I was starting to work on my Easter series *Extravagant Love*, I purchased it. I love John Ortberg. I know that he offers solid Bible teaching, relevant illustrations, and current applications of truth. I anticipate smiling and even laughing out loud. I know that he will make me think of ideas from a different perspective, and I can expect several good quotes for my series. How do I know this? I know Ortberg's brand.

> "Human beings have [always] been a part of one tribe or another. A group needs only two things to be a tribe: a shared interest and a way to communicate."
> Seth Godin

What's the Big Deal?

You will have a brand whether you know it or not. Readers will create a brand in their minds that fits you. Do you think their brand will depict you the way you want to be seen? You should ask yourself this. *Do you want to build your brand, or would you rather let your brand build you?*

In a sense, your brand will define you. No matter what you write or how well you write, it is best to build your brand on the front end. Knowing your brand not only helps you market your books but also helps you to know what to write in the first place. As an author and president of Novel Publicity, Emlyn Chand experienced the highs and lows of successful and not so successful marketing. She discovered, after the fact, the importance of firmly establishing her brand as an author. She said, "Discovering your brand is about discovering what you offer that readers love."[4] Chand created a workbook to help authors discover their brand, and I highly recommend it.

> *"To be in business today, our most important job is to be head marketer for the brand called You."*
> Tom Peters

I spend nearly as much time in sermon preparation thinking about what *not* to say as about what *to* say. I know that unless God really moves on a Sunday morning, I need to fit my message into an allotted time period, which I struggle to do. Too many times, preachers blame God for long sermons when the fault lies in poor planning. The same is true in our writing. I have ideas for books all of the time. I have only one life to live and so many books to write. I need to decide what I will write just as much as what I shouldn't write. Determining my brand will help me weed out the topics I should ignore.

If we write books about every topic under the sun that have no connection, we will build a scattered following. Imagine the disappointment your reader may experience if your first book was a home run on leadership development, and your second book was on how to potty train your pre-schooler. They might be disappointed if they purchased your second book without investigating the content, especially if their interest was in leadership development.

Decision Time

Making choices about our brands may be a difficult process. In my case, as a pastor or Bible teacher, I find that I have more freedom than other authors. As a Bible teacher, my mission is to unveil God's truth on a variety of topics. My writing can reflect this mission. You could still say my brand centers around biblical principles for a meaningful life.

People want to hear from the pastor on a variety of topics. I have people ask me about different issues and what the Bible has to say about them. I invariably preach or teach through books of the Bible as well as share biblical principles on life issues. I do not think that anyone is surprised that I have written a book on the Psalms, Proverbs, and Bible prophecy. I started a new series of shorter books entitled "Reading the Bible." I plan to write books on how to get the most out of reading various sections of the Bible. I started with Psalms: *How to Get the Most out of Reading Psalms*. If you're interested, I am offering it as a gift to people who purchase my first book on Psalms: *Songs from the Heart*, but you are welcome to it as well by visiting timriordan.com.

I may be a bad example of this entire topic of carefully selecting a brand. I am a Bible teacher and a pastor, and I have written books on biblical themes as well as on how to write and publish. I have also written a number of fiction books, though I choose to use a pen name. I will address this option below. I have chosen to expand my brand to help people write and publish because I want to help people share messages of hope and redemption.

How to Determine Your Brand

If you had one message, what would it be? This one is difficult for me to nail down. I have chosen to write fiction for secular readers in hopes of gently presenting biblical truths about relationships and life. In a way, writing fiction for me is my hobby. It's what I do on the side for fun and relaxation. I do not usually watch TV or play golf, though I enjoy both. Instead, I write. My fiction has become my mental vacation, and I'm hoping to influence readers to consider spiritual truths through fun stories about relationships and adventure.

My novels are different from my books on Bible teaching or writing, so I use a pen name. I also have a suspicion that some people will have preconceived ideas about a romance/suspense/action novel written by a pastor. Some of their ideas will be true. I don't include graphic scenes or use foul language. However, my approach is to introduce spiritual themes and offer an engaging story that shows readers how life and love can be experienced. Time will tell if I am able to influence people with this strategy.

> "Your personal brand is what people say about you when you are not in the room."
>
> Chris Ducker

Because I use a pen name for my fiction, I think I have two brands. Maintaining two different personas is a challenge, but hopefully, it will bear fruit. To determine my brand, I decided to first work on developing a personal mission and ministry statement: *My purpose for writing is to lead people to have a passionate and growing relationship with Jesus Christ.* This purpose statement leaves a wide door open for a variety of topics. In a general way, it also influences my novels.

> "You are not a product of your circumstances but a product of your decisions."
> Stephen Covey

The problem we face is that we could write a million books that fulfill our purposes. Therefore, we have to go back to the first question of this section: If you had one message to share, what would it be? Answering this question may narrow your topics down to a manageable brand.

Also consider your background, education, experience, and passions. I have always heard that we should "write what we know." I have a doctorate in ministry, and I have taught the Bible most of my life. Although I have much to learn about the Bible, I can write about my journey so far. I am also a scuba diver, and I find that readers enjoy imagining participating in the sport without ever getting wet. These two concepts influence my nonfiction and fiction writing.

How do you want to be remembered? What themes or topics are "must tells" before you die? If you could pass along one message to your children and grandchildren, what would it be? Who is your typical reader? You should carefully create a picture or description of your typical reader. Answering these questions will help you determine your brand. I will address this more in the next chapter.

All of these questions and considerations will also help you narrow your topic. Once you have decided whom you will present to your readers and what topics you plan to cover, you will have to determine *how* to build your brand. This step may involve websites, color choices, logos, and an advertising strategy. Your brand will be shaped by what you write and how you present yourself in your bio and your public speaking. It could affect where you advertise and with whom you work on future books. I recommend you consider this topic and read what other writers have to say about building your brand.

> *"Networking is an enrichment program, not an entitlement program."*
> Susan RoAne

You may never have given the concept of brand a thought, but it is important. Businesses and churches are affected by the brand offered. I am a Bible teacher, and I know my preaching style is affected by my gifts and passion to teach God's Word. This passion shapes my brand as a pastor and determines, in some ways, who will come to my church.

Whom does your brand impact? *Considering the "whom" will help you create the "what."* Let's look at that topic next.

Action Points

- Have you ever connected branding to the success of an author? Can you list four reasons why creating a brand is important for an author's success?

- I said that branding is both a noun and verb. Can you see how it both defines you and it is something you do? Jot down a few notes on how it can be both in your writing career.
- Why do you need a brand? Can you list several reasons?
- Have you written out a purpose statement as an author? If not, do so now.
- Make a list of the things, ideas, stories, or truths about which you are really passionate. How might that be used in your brand?
- How would you express your brand in your logo, author picture, or writing style?
- What difference will your brand make in your marketing decisions and strategy?

Chapter Six

Know Thy Readers

Cooking shows have grown in popularity over the last few years. According to *Marketing Charts*, eight in ten adults watch cooking shows.[1] Another cooking phenomenon that has grown in popularity is cooking contests. I have learned that cooks who compete also choose to guard their recipes closely. It seems many cooks have some secret ingredient that takes their cuisine to blue-ribbon status.

I want to share something in this chapter that could be the secret ingredient to successful writing and marketing. Although the focus of this book is on marketing, I include writing because once you work through this chapter and accept some of the information, these concepts will affect how you write. The only problem with the content of this chapter is that it will go against much of what you believe and have accepted to be part of your call to write. I do not suggest you throw away your convictions, but I do think the principles I share will help you be a better writer and marketer.

It's Not About You

Rick Warren began his life-changing book *What On Earth Am I Here For?* (formerly *The Purpose Driven Life*) with these arresting words: "It's not about you."[2] One of the great realities and fallacies of the human race is that we believe the world revolves around us. Hopefully, as we have matured, we realize that what God thinks is what matters most, and other people are more important than ourselves.

One problem we face in response to self-orientation is we make decisions based upon our own motivations and preferences. For example, we may choose to write a certain book because it deals with a topic of our own interests. In marketing, we may decide to market a certain way because we like a particular method.

> "I alone cannot change the world, but I can cast a stone across the water to create many ripples."
> Mother Teresa

A friend who writes told me that she refused to get onto Facebook because she hated it. Thousands, even millions, of potential readers are on Facebook every day, but because of her resolve, she is missing them.

If *it's not about you*, then you will have to step into the minds of readers in order to figure out how to connect with them through the writing and marketing of your book. This process may require you to develop some disciplines and habits in regard to marketing that you do not enjoy; however, you will market because your message is important.

If my friend really wants to get her message out to the public, she should consider spending five minutes a day on Facebook. She'd be doing something she doesn't like so that she can connect with thousands of potential readers, which is something she would like. She may eventually sell hundreds of books to new readers.

I once read that Tom Landry, legendary former coach for the Dallas Cowboys, said, "Leadership is getting someone to do what they don't want to do to achieve what they want to achieve." If we want to successfully market our books, we may have to do something we don't want to do to achieve what we do want to achieve.

Since *it's not about you*, it *is* about your audience. We can view this concept from two perspectives. My first perspective, which is influenced by my faith, leads me to see that I have an audience of one: God.

Song writer Greg Ferguson put this principle into proper perspective:

> *I'll be content to serve an audience of One*
> *Only His approval counts when all is said and done*
> *And this is my prayer, when the race is finally run*
> *I want to hear "Well done" from the audience of One.*[3]

When all is said and done (or written), only one opinion matters: God's! As a Christian writer, my ultimate goal is God's glory. Think about how this understanding affects the way we market. First, it will be a motivation *to* market because we want people everywhere to read the message God has placed upon our hearts.

As in any area of life, our desire to please God may affect *where* and *how* we market. You may have an opportunity to market your book through an avenue that would not represent your convictions. Even as we submit our writing process to God, we should also submit our marketing practices to Him.

God is our main audience, and that reality should be our overarching motivation. We must also be sensitive about how to write and market in a way as to have the greatest impact on people. This reality leads us to the second perspective we should consider.

We write for others and not ourselves, and our mission is to be used by God to change lives. I love to write, but my reason must always be for the benefit of others. This understanding requires me to consider my audience as I create my marketing plan.

Counterculture

Everyone exists within a culture, and life and ministry have their own set of cultural norms. Allow me to share something from a Christian perspective. As a Christian and a minister, one of those norms that has a strong biblical base is that we are called to spread the message of the gospel to everyone. Because the Great Commission is ingrained into our psyche, we feel compelled to write and market our books for everyone. I realize that not everyone reading this book is a Christian, but the principle remains the same. Earlier, I reminded you *it's not about you!* In this section, you're going to see *it's not about everyone else* either.

I admit this concept is hard for me to accept. Many authors have the opinion that they write books for everyone on the planet. Not so.

Unfortunately, not everyone will read your book or want to read anything you write. Your writing will attract a certain type of reader based upon various factors including style, content, and length. Readers will also be attracted to you as a writer based upon your experiences, education, or genre. Although you want everyone to read your books, the fact is that you can predict a number of things about the kind of person who will be drawn to your writing. These predictions can become the basis for a strong marketing strategy.

Marketing strategy is not a "one size fits all" proposition. A writer's approach will be different based upon his or her audience. For example, if your typical reader is a college student, email marketing may not have as much effect as Instagram. College students are not as faithful to email but use social media regularly. According to a Pew Research report, 90% of young adults are using social media with 55% using Instagram at least once a day.[4] If you send out an email about a special promotion you're running, they *may* see it a month after the promotion ended. But, if you take an engaging picture and send it out on Instagram, you are more likely to have an instant response from that demographic.

The Power of Focus

Focus is an amazing key to success. Author Jack Canfield (co-author of *Chicken Soup for the Soul*) stated, "The number one reason that stops people from getting what they want is lack of focus."[5] The principle of focus applies to every area of life including business, finances, ministry, relationships, writing—everything. When Steve Jobs came back to Apple as CEO in 1997, he led the company to eliminate 70 percent of the product line. He believed Apple would flourish if leaders chose to streamline their company. Instead of offering many options, they decided to focus on a few. The rest is history.[6]

By carefully defining your target, you are creating focus for your marketing strategy. Instead of spending a lot of money on many strategies, focus your marketing on areas that will have the greatest impact on people who are most likely to read your book. In Chapter Two, I asked you to consider the difference between light from a light bulb and that from a laser beam. A light bulb illuminates steel, but a laser beam cuts through it. When you determine who your readers are before you write and market, your effect will be like a laser beam as you cut through barriers to real needs in the lives of your readers.

Defining Your Market

In my book, *How to Write and Publish Books*, I mentioned the concept of creating a demographic and psycho-graphic profile of your typical reader. I highly recommend this practice. Creating a profile of who may be drawn to your book is the "secret sauce" in your recipe for gourmet marketing and writing.

Michael Hyatt offers a great summary to help you define your market in *Writing a Winning Nonfiction Book Proposal.* This resource is a guide to helping writers create a proposal to send a publisher, and one step includes defining your market. He reveals that defining your market includes several topics: demographics, psychographics, affinity groups, and related material.[7]

Understanding the demographic of your market includes determining the age range, sex, socio-economic background, educational background, and religious background of your potential reader. Recently, I applied for a promotion through a new advertising source, but the owner graciously wrote back and told me that religious books did not typically fare well through his company. If I conclude that my normal reader is a Christian in the age range of 35 – 55, I should not advertise with a company that doesn't connect with Christians in that age range. Knowing the demographic of your potential readers will keep you from wasting money on advertising that's not effective.

Having a psychographic profile of your readers will help you understand the motivations that lead people to purchase your book. This type of profile will help you know how your potential readers feel. It may help you determine their passions and frustrations, and it will guide you in designing your advertisement

> "Readers have to be sought out and won to the light of the page."
> C. D. Wright

pieces and choosing promotional services.

Next, consider the kinds of groups to which your readers relate or belong. Do your readers join book clubs or attend Parents of Preschoolers meetings? Do they like networks such as Fox News, or do they usually watch CBN? If you want to connect with potential readers, it is best to go to where they are instead of expecting them to come to you. You can find people "hanging out" in all kinds of groups online. If you want to connect to Christians who like to study the Bible, find a Facebook group of Christian Bible students.

If you write books that predominately connect with women, you may want to create visuals that can be pinned to Pinterest. If your audience has a strong business background, LinkedIn is a good focal point for you. If your potential readers are frustrated by parenting woes, consider creating a blog for young parents.

Finally, what other resources are available in your particular field? Does anyone else blog on the topic of your book? Join different blogs that deal with your topic and interact with potential readers. Follow other similar authors and emulate some of their strategy points.

Engaging Your Market

I must point out a foundational concept that will change your marketing strategy. People are selfish. I realize we all know this fact but consider it from a marketing perspective. No one wants to buy your book to help your sales numbers or send your kids to college. *People will buy your books if your books will help make their lives better.* Everyone's number one question when considering a purchase is "What's in it for me?"

For example, when people find out that you're an author, they typically respond with something like, "So, you're an author. What kind of books do you write?" They don't care about what kind of books you write. What they're asking is, "Do you write anything that will help me?" When someone asks about my novels, I say, "I write stories that help my readers experience the kind of relationships they've always dreamed of having."

Think about this concept from a marketing strategy. Because people are concerned about their needs or desires and want to know if our books will do something positive for them, we should market by showing them how our books will change their lives. Think of marketing from your readers' perspective.

The goal of knowing your market is to engage them. Through engagement, potential readers will buy your book and be influenced by it. The main message is that if you do not know your market, you cannot engage them.

After you spend time working through the exercises that help you understand your potential readers, you will be ready to begin putting together the pieces of the marketing puzzle. The next chapter introduces you to methods you can follow that lead to marketing success.

Action Points

- Why do you write? Take a moment to write (or rewrite) your purpose statement as a writer.
- Now that you have considered your purpose, write out a mission statement that incorporates the audience you are trying to reach.
- How might the *Audience of One* concept affect your writing and marketing?
- Do you find it difficult to accept that your audience is probably not everyone? Have you considered that Jesus did not heal all of the lepers or restore sight to all of the blind? How might understanding your audience give you focus in marketing?
- You may find Michael Hyatt's short ebook on creating a proposal helpful. Visit his website (michaelhyatt.com) and note the relevant resources.
- Spend time writing out a profile of your typical reader. Make a list of how understanding your reader will impact your marketing.

Chapter Seven

Creating a Marketing Strategy

I remember the day I began my first pastorate. I became a lead pastor after my nineteenth birthday. It's hard for me to think of myself as the "senior pastor" at nineteen, but I was, and I was clueless about life and ministry. If you had been hiding in the corner behind the fake ficus tree, you would have seen me ease into the pastor's study that first Monday morning. I sat behind the desk and sheepishly looked around at my empty bookshelves. After several minutes of quiet that made me feel more like a mortician than a pastor, I asked out loud, "Now, what do I do?"

You may be feeling the way I did so many years ago. One problem I experienced was I didn't have anyone to help me figure out my next move. What I would have given for an older pastor/mentor at that time! Maybe I can be a mentor for you in the area of marketing. Although I am still a student, and I am still learning new techniques, I will do my best to guide you down the path of marketing your book.

Small Steps

In a previous chapter, I mentioned the principle of small steps. Instant, success is not the rule but rather the exception. *Most of the time, success is the result of consistent, intentional small steps strung together over time.* The question is "What are the steps?" If you are going to market your book successfully, you must take several steps that involve effort, determination, and creativity.

Shelley Hitz has been one of my mentors in self-publishing, and she, along with Heather Hart, wrote *Book Marketing Success Bundle*. In the first section of the book, which is now available as a single ebook entitled *Book Marketing Success for Beginners*, Heather compared the challenge of marketing your book to a spider weaving a web.[1] The more strands you weave, the greater the opportunity for marketing success. As you consider weaving together steps in successful marketing, you see the strands of a growing web.

One strand may be more essential than another, but you will discover your marketing strategy has a synergistic effect on book sales. Can one strand of webbing catch dinner for a spider? I am no spider expert, but I suppose it could happen. If I were a spider, however, I would build a web of multiple strands in one location. I would then franchise my web services out to have greater opportunities for many sumptuous meals.

Don't Just Stand There

Don't just stand there; do something. It's easy to become overwhelmed by all the options or strands in your web and to be stymied into inactivity. Options are wonderful, but sometimes we consider all the possibilities and find ourselves doing nothing at all. It's like trying to choose a box of cereal at the grocery store from scores of different possibilities. If we are not careful, we find ourselves standing there making no progress.

I once heard John Maxwell say, "If you always do what you've always done, you'll always get what you've always got." The principle behind this quote is what moved me out of the lethargy of wanting to be a writer into the victory ring of a published author. I couldn't continue standing around evaluating the options. I had to act. When I realized that doing nothing would not make me a published author, I started doing something.

This sluggishness will not just keep you from being a writer; it will keep you from being a successful writer. You did not write a book just so you could say you are an author. Your goal must be to write books people will purchase, read, and apply. If you are sluggish about marketing, your goal will never be realized.

Keep in mind the something you do at first might not be the something you continue to do. In building a marketing strategy, some of the construction will take place through trial and error. Life is that way. How many people do you know who are happily working in a career for which they were prepared by receiving their college degrees? Many people receive degrees in particular fields only to discover they do not enjoy that vocation. After a few experimental careers, they finally land on the work they love doing.

> "Winners were not born winners; they learnt and practiced how to win."
> Israelmore Ayivor

Be willing to try different strategies. You may start out working to become a Twitter expert only to discover what really works best for you is blogging. My advice is simply to start somewhere. While I believe a few strands of the marketing web are essential, there is flexibility when it comes to promoting your book.

Although you must do something, you do not have to do everything. So, let's figure out your first step!

Building Blocks of Your Marketing Strategy

Whether you are comfortable with the imagery of a web or prefer the visual of a building's foundation, an effective strategy will be multifaceted. As a web has many strands and a foundation has many blocks, your marketing strategy will not be successful unless you utilize multiple aspects to your overall plan. I have listed a few key strands to your overall marketing design. Some of these *strands* may be viewed as essential while others are optional. I will discuss some of these in further detail in the following chapters.

- Website – You will see in the next chapter that your website will become the hub of your entire marketing strategy. Everything you do should direct people back to your website, for it is through this central hub that you will be able to communicate with your readers.
- Blog – Writing a regular blog will enable you to interact with a broad spectrum of people, and it will provide you a means by which you can gain followers through the help of your readers. I just wrote a blog yesterday and saw through social media that it had been shared many times, bringing many new readers to my site.
- Social Media – Like it or not, social media (Facebook, Twitter, Pinterest, LinkedIn, etc.) is here to stay. Though platforms may change, people want to be able to interact with others through technological channels. Social media can become an author's best friend; you just have to learn how to use it.

- Book Reviews – I never wrote a review until I became an author, but I read many of them before choosing various products. I now know how essential good reviews are to the success of my books.

- Face-to-Face – This part of the strategy includes speaking engagements, book signings, and other guest appearances where authors can physically interact with readers.

- Media – Radio interviews, newspaper articles, television appearances, and magazine articles are ways authors can tap into the media strand of the marketing web.

- Video – The call for video marketing is growing. YouTube and other video driven platforms have grown in popularity, calling authors to consider the impact of this market stream. Experts predict a steady growth in this medium, so authors should determine a means by which they can tap into video marketing. In *Build Your Author Platform*, former editor Carole Jelen and tech expert Michael McCallister wrote, "Visitors who view product videos are 85% *more likely to buy* than visitors who do not..."[2] That statistic should encourage you to look into how to connect with prospective readers through video.

- Internet Marketing – This method can include internet blasts or an advertisement blitz through online marketers. I have used this method to some level of success, but you can also connect to ready readers by increasing your own email database, engaging in click ads on Facebook or Amazon, or purchasing other online advertising. Sometimes, internet marketing is free, but you may find a little investment can go a long way.

- Amazon – Though Amazon is a retailer of many products, including books, it also provides a wonderful marketing tool. I addressed this in a previous book on performing keyword searches.
- Building a Team – Do not market alone. As your publishing efforts are greatly enhanced through a team, so is your marketing strategy.

In the following chapters, I plan to help you sort through some of the options and determine which steps are best for you. While my information will not be comprehensive, I think it will help you choose a few marketing building blocks that will offer a strong platform from which to promote your book. I urge you to become a lifelong student of marketing and find other great resources to help you.

The Goal of the Marketing Strategy

The goal of our marketing strategy should be simple. Right? Sell more books? Wrong! Hopefully your ambition to become a writer was not to sell books. We became authors because we believe that we have the most important message in the entire world to give our readers. Both fiction and non-fiction writers want to influence readers to learn, grow, serve, relax, or laugh. Whether our goal is to instruct or entertain, we want to take readers on a journey. God has called us to use every method possible to impact the lives of people, and one of those methods is writing.

If life change is your goal, other people will be your focus. When I run into an author or ministry leader whose favorite topic is himself, his last book, or his last sermon, I'm turned off. Years ago, I heard someone say, "People don't care how much you know until they know how much you care." If you really care about people, then your concerns must come through in your marketing strategy. If people feel as if they are being used to build someone else's bank account, your impact will be short-lived. Your marketing strategy can either move you forward into being used by God to change lives or lead you to the one-book club oblivion.

Don't misunderstand me. We want to sell books because that means more people are being impacted by our message. We must be careful, however, and never portray the idea that we are book hustlers. Instead, we are change agents.

What Now?

Learning about marketing strategy is like taking a drink out of a fire hydrant. Don't be discouraged and over-whelmed. I urge you to read each of these chapters, study other resources, and pick two or three areas that you will master. I suggest in the next chapter that one of those areas should be an author website, but your strategy will always be a work in progress. Start small and build. Avoid the temp-tation of doing ten marketing ideas poorly. Do three or four of them well.

As you review steps toward gaining readers, consider several ideas, such as time, gifts, and personality. If you are an introvert who trembles at the thought of saying a word in a small group of friends, then public speaking might not be first on your list of strategies. If you are a pastor, business leader, or Bible study leader, public speaking is your forte, so maybe it should be near the top of your list. Your challenge may be determining how to utilize your gift and plan events with the time constraints your fulltime job presents.

Okay, so where do you start? I've already mentioned that your author website should be your marketing hub, so let's look at this key building block. When I became serious about writing, I knew nothing about designing a website. Don't let your lack of knowledge on this topic cause you not to turn the page and read the next chapter.

Action Points

- Consider the two images I presented: a web and a foundation. Which of these do you think best fits the idea of designing a marketing strategy?

- Do you find it difficult to deal with defeat? Error doesn't have to be a bad thing. Thomas Edison reportedly said, "I have not failed. I have just found 1000 ways that won't work." Are you willing to create a strategy for marketing while knowing that your strategy will present the opportunity for learning "ways that won't work"?

- Look over the list of ten marketing ideas or building blocks. Which of these do you think will come easy? Which do you think are more challenging?

- What about creating an author website? Are you willing to follow a step-by-step guide in accomplishing this task?

- Do you use social media now? If so, how might your platform be helpful in gaining interest in current or future books?

- Do reviews ever sway you in making or not making a purchase? Have you ever written a review for a book or a product? Why or why not? Will you please write a review for this book? I'd be grateful.

- What is your goal for marketing your book? Write out a brief marketing purpose statement.

Chapter Eight

Constructing Your Author Website

In this chapter, I'll introduce to you the first essential strand to marketing success. I'll share additional strands in following chapters, but right now let's consider creating a strong foundation for your marketing experience.

As foundations are important to a house, your author website is critical for marketing your book and expanding your influence or ministry. An article in *Writer's Digest* reported, "An author website is your most critical tool for book promotion and long-term platform development."[1] Some authors see social media as their most critical tool. Your success through social media, however, is up to other people while you have control of your website.

You may consider your website as the main strand of your web or a hub for your writing career. It becomes the central point from which every other strand will begin. Some of you already feel defeated because you believe having a website is an impossible feat. Creating a website, however, is not impossible. If you have no experience in website design, a lot of options exist to help you accomplish this goal. You may be surprised at the number of resources available that will assist a novice at creating a functional website. You

> *"A website is a window through which your business says hello to the world."*
> Amit Kalantri

will need to learn how to develop a website or pay someone
to do it for you.

Knowing the Language

I had to build my own website because I didn't have
money to pay someone else to do it. I went into the task of
website development with the opinion that if someone else
could do it, so could I. The wonderful news is you do not
have to be a professional computer programmer to create a
useful website. Before going into the details of creating and
using a website, I'd like to share with you a few key terms
you need to understand.

• Domain – The domain is the name used to identify your
  website. It is the URL or Web address people type into
  a browser search window to find you. Most authors use
  their names, but others use the name of their book. If
  you plan to write more than one book, I suggest you use
  your name. My domain was originally timriordan.me. I
  preferred to use a .com domain name, but unfortunately
  timriordan.com was a premium site and would have cost
  around $1600 a few years ago. I eventually added tim
  riordan.net. Recently, timriordan.com dropped in price,
  so I purchased it, too. I point all of my domains to the
  same website, so I don't have three different sites. You
  can locate a domain name by visiting the website of a
  hosting service. They have a feature that enables you to
  review options for naming your website. I suggest using
  your name, if possible. Your name is your brand.

• Web Host – Web hosting is a service that makes your
  site available for the public. Some people use free services for hosting, such as WordPress or Blogger, but I

suggest you pay a little so you can have complete flexibility. I find it best to use a combination of services like WordPress and a host service like Bluehost or Go-Daddy. Some authors choose a premium hosting service which provides security, backups, and great support. I have opted for the premium service with WordPress because I do not want advertisements on my site. It's possible to start with the basic service offered by Word-Press that is free and later transition to a self-hosting service that has a minimal monthly fee.

You should still purchase your own domain name, but you could get by initially without having to pay for hosting. As of this writing, one great advantage of using Bluehost is that it offers a premium version of Word-Press for free, and the hosting cost is reasonable. Word-Press is the most popular and easiest blogging/website content management system available. It's restrictive if you have a specific design in mind because you have to use their design themes.

My personal websites (timriordan.com and judah knight. com) use WordPress so I can blog, among other things. For my publishing website (greentreepublishers. com), I use a website design program offered by Go-Daddy where I can create the page I want. I have to pay an annual fee for this extra service. Bluehost is my host for judahknight.com.

- Browser – I'm assuming that you understand a browser is the software-based program you use to access the internet. I mention it here because you need to consider other people's browsers as you set up your website. Your website may function perfectly in Google Chrome but not look so good in Firefox. You can use a service like Brow-ser Shots to check cross compatibility for multiple browsers.

- E-Commerce – Electronic Commerce is the process of buying and selling online. You might consider adding an e-commerce function to your website as your customer base grows. Most of your sales will probably come through Amazon or another retailer, but it's possible you may be interested in making sales from your website. So far, I do not.

- HTML – This acronym stands for Hypertext Markup Language, and it is the language used by programmers to write websites. The good news is you do not have to be proficient in the language in order to create a website. You may, however, find it helpful along the way to pick up on a few codes you can insert. Working with HTML requires an HTML editor. When I write my blog, I have the option of choosing a visual editor or a text editor. The text option shows the code used within my blog. If I wanted to add a space and for some reason pressing the enter button did not do it for me, I could add the code <br>. This means to add a break. I found this helpful in setting up my description on Amazon when it would not read my space commands.

- Hyperlink – If you are reading the digital version of this book, you have already seen numerous hyperlinks. A hyperlink is a link from one webpage to another or from one place in a document to another place in the same document. The table of contents of this book in the digital format is an internal hyperlink taking you from the contents page to the particular designated place in the book. An external link will take you to another website. You will recognize a hyperlink by the under-lined word in blue.

- Landing Page – This term refers to the first page of your website people visit when they type in your domain name. This page is critical to the success of your site in that people may only give you a few seconds to catch their attention. You should also include some type of call to action on this page, which could be asking them to sign up for your newsletter, sign up for a free gift, or pur-chase your book.

- Plugin – A plugin is a mini-program or third-party code you can add to your website. WordPress offers a number of plugins that extend website capabilities. On my site, I have one used for signing up for my newsletter, for giv-ing me statistics on how many people visit my site, and for sharing my site on social media.

Important Website Elements

When you begin designing your webpage, it's like you are sitting before a blank canvas and preparing to paint a picture. The advantage of using WordPress or another ser-vice that helps you build your site, is they provide templates that make setting up your site easier. You may still feel like you are painting a picture, but at least you are now "painting by numbers" instead of creating your masterpiece from scratch. The negative side of this feature is the offered tem-plate may be restrictive.

As you consider your blank canvas, you may be wondering what should be included. I suggest you first make notes on what you want included in your website and even draw basic models of each page. Consider the following suggestions for various pages of your site.

- Landing Page – Your opening page must be engaging and offer a call to action. I suggest you include your blog as a small piece of your opening page so as to encourage return guests. It may offer only a title and a few sentences requiring them to click a link to read all of your comments. You should also include a good picture of yourself with a byline that contains a very brief introduction of yourself, your mission, or your ministry.

  Your tabs leading to other pages will also be visible, so think carefully about what these tabs should be. I suggest including a newsletter sign up or at least a sign up to join your blog. You need a way to correspond with your readers and invite them to additional levels of participation. Links to your book(s) should be on the landing page along with opportunities for readers to share your site through social media.

  One critical addition should be included on your landing page that I'll cover in detail in another chapter. You should offer a gift that requires your readers to share their email addresses. Many authors will tell you email marketing is the most effective tool in their toolbox, so consider the benefits carefully.

- Blog – I prefer to include my blog on my website. Part of the reason for this preference is it keeps my website fresh with new information. It calls readers to return to my site often when I update my blog. Some authors add it as a tab on their landing page, but I prefer to have the blog included on the first page. I want my readers to visit my website often for updates and consider additional calls to action I may include. When I add a new blog, all my subscribers automatically receive an email inviting them to come to my website to read my newest comments.

> *"Unrelatability is the kiss of death for many pieces of writing."*
> Loren

- Bio Page – You should have a brief bio on your landing page and provide additional information about yourself later in your website. Remember we live in the day of social media, and your readers want to feel like they are your friends. You may consider adding a biographical video as well. I'll cover this topic briefly in my chapter on video marketing.

   Knowing about your family, your background, your likes, and your dislikes helps your readers to feel they have inside knowledge to your life. Readers want to personally connect Include a few pictures as well as things that qualify you to write. Those qualifications may simply be your passion for your topic or your desire to encourage people. It may include your educational background or your places of service or employment.

- Media Page – I suggest one of your tabs be something for media personnel. You are hoping to have represen- tatives from newspapers or radio stations interested in writing about you or interviewing you. A media page can offer background information about your book or about your life that will help them write the story. I also include suggested interview questions. The media personnel will be more likely to include an article about your new book if you make their jobs easier by providing information. Later on, I'll write about a media kit, and you'll find this media tab is the foundation piece of the kit.

- Contact Information – Do not make it difficult for an interested reader or member of the media to discover how to get in touch with you. The days of hiding behind a closed door and keeping your contact information private are gone. People want to connect with you.

    Although you may want to limit what information you share, people want to interact with you. This inform- ation should include an email address, a mailing address (though you should use a post office box), and possibly a phone number. I suggest you sign up for a Gmail account and take advantage of the free phone number they offer you. The Google number can be connected to your cell phone, and it rings on your phone just like any other call. The advantage is that you are not giving out your personal phone number. When you answer a call from your Google account, you are given the option to answer the call or send it to voice mail.

- Information on your Books – Make sure you include links to where your book(s) can be purchased. Even though you can purchase my books from any retailer, I use a link to Amazon on my website. I also have a separate page that offers more detail on my books. I include endorsements from recognizable names as well as a few of my better reviews from Amazon.

- Links – I think it's good to add links to other websites where your readers can be encouraged or where they can learn more about topics discussed in your books. It is especially important to offer links to places like your church's website (if you're a pastor or church leader), your business website (if you're a business leader), a page where your readers can listen to your sermons (if you preach regularly) or podcasts, your publisher's website (if you have one), your Goodreads page (you should check out Goodreads.com), and any other website that deals with your ministry or writing career.

What's Next?

Now you realize you need a website as a basis for your marketing strategy, but what do you do with that information? First, you need a domain name, so I suggest you visit a site like bluehost.com/track/considerbluehost, hostgator.com, or godaddy.com and begin the process of getting a domain and securing a host.

After securing a domain and a hosting service, you need to make decisions about integrating WordPress or another service with your website. I've only had experience with two different blogging services, but I recommend WordPress. It provides an easy process of creating a website, which includes a blog, through the use of a variety of different templates. Michael Hyatt offers a useful resource that will guide you through the process of setting up your website by integrating it with WordPress.[2] It is entitled "How to Launch a Self-Hosted WordPress Blog in 20 Minutes or Less—A Step-by-Step Guide."

What other things should you include in your marketing web? In the next chapter, we'll cover the important strand of your web called social media. I became a bestselling author on Amazon, and a lot of my success came through the use of social media. Look at the next chapter, and I'll tell you how I did it.

Action Points

- How have you experienced success in other areas of your life through the principle of small steps?
- Look at some author websites and make notes of the things you like about the site. Consider looking at the websites of Randy Alcorn, Nancy Leigh DeMoss, John Eldredge, Ann VosKamp, and Michael Hyatt. Check out my website at timriordan.com.
- I suggested you take your first step in creating your marketing web by developing a website. Take a moment to write out a plan for your proposed website. You can always make changes to it later, but first decide how you want your website to look when it's complete.
- Sign up for a domain name, hosting service, and WordPress account through one of the hosting services I suggested (Bluehost, Hostgator, or iPage) or through another service of your choice.
- Choose a template through WordPress and take the initial steps to set up your account.

- Make sure you look at your finished website on computers and mobile devices. It needs to be optimized for devices such as iPhones and iPads.

What Authors Should Consider when Choosing a Hosting Service

Initial Decisions

- Will you include a blog?
- Will you need to purchase a domain name?
- Do you plan to sell books from your website?
- Do you anticipate having multiple websites?
- How many email addresses will you need?
- Do you need a basic author site, or do you have big plans to expand into a larger business in the future?

Contributing Factors to your Final Decision

Type

When people first begin looking into hosting services, they may read information regarding the type of site they need. For example, if you're going to open up a high-traffic site where you'll be selling multiple items, you don't want your site sitting on a server along with other websites. This could slow your site down. Your options include shared hosting, VPS (Virtual Private Server), or dedicated hosting. As an author, however, you don't need to have a dedicated server or even a virtual private server. It's cheaper and just as effective to use a shared server for your website. If you plan to become the next Amazon, you should opt for a dedicated service.

Simplicity

Most of us are not web designers who are proficient with coding. Unless you are good with HTML and CSS codes, you'll want a website that's easy to design and intuitive. While searching for a hosting service, you'll find a spectrum from where you can purchase a predesigned template to where you can individually design the whole site. I like the website builder services that a company like GoDaddy, Wix, or Squarespace offers, but I don't like having to pay for it. I can't speak to costs related to Wix or Squarespace, but I have personal experience with GoDaddy. I like WordPress, but I find that design is not intuitive or simple. Once you figure it out, however, web design is not a big deal, and it's a good option if you plan to blog. For this reason, I switched to Bluehost and use WordPress. You can find several good WordPress themes that give you the "drag and drop" flexibility of a website builder program, but they cost additional money. I plan to use one of those themes on the website to promote this book. I know some people who use Wix and are very satisfied with its simplicity. My son uses Squarespace and is very satisfied. I found an excellent review of Wix you may want to consider. You can find it by visiting shivarweb.com/4794/wix-review.

Flexibility

Can you do what you want to do on your website? That question should be on your mind as you choose a company. Of course, you first have to know what you want your site to accomplish. As an author, I want to write a blog, promote my books, have multiple tabs where I can offer special promotions for my books, and possibly offer ecommerce services so people can buy my books from my website. I don't sell my books from my site at this time. I simply send them to a retailer like Amazon or Barnes & Noble through a hyperlink. I don't want roadblocks when I'm trying to create something for my site, so flexibility is key. I also want to be able to expand sometime in the future and possibly add ecommerce to my site, especially my publishing site at greentreepublishers.com.

Customer Support

You'll need customer support somewhere along the way, so you want a service that actually serves its customers. I have found that GoDaddy offers excellent customer service through both online help as well as telephone availability. I've also been satisfied with Bluehost, though I've not had as much need for customer service. I found a great comparison of hosting services offered by PC Magazine and written by Jeffrey Wilson in October of 2019. At the bottom of the article, Wilson compares several companies and includes comments about customer support. Visit pcmag.com/roundup/316108/the-best-web-hosting-services to check out this useful resource.

Cost

Cost isn't everything, but it is something. I'm willing to pay a little more each month for needed services, but I will also consider cost in my final decision. The first issue you'll need to consider is the promotional fee versus the annual renewal. A lot of companies will offer a discount for the first year of service, but then upon renewal, your price will go up. Be ready for this change. Secondly, some companies charge fees for every service they offer (email addresses, website builder, etc.). When comparing sites, make sure you're including all of the fees. I switched from GoDaddy to Bluehost for several reasons, but one those was because Bluehost offers me all of the email addresses I want for free. GoDaddy charged for email addresses. Thirdly, don't forget to include charges for your domain name and for security. It's worth paying extra to keep your name and phone number out of the public eye. I didn't do this at first, and my cell phone rings multiple times a day with promotions that I'm confident came because of my exposure through my websites. The bottom line on cost is that you can get good service for less than five dollars per month, or no more than ten dollars.

Chapter Nine

Social Media

I have to confess that I fought social media for a while, but in the end, social media won. It seems silly to report to the world our trips to Walmart to get a gallon of milk or that we just had a funny thought while driving to church. I felt most people don't care about that kind of information, but evidently, I was wrong. Social media (SM) offers more than an opportunity to inform the world of my shopping adventures; it offers an opportunity to connect.

The fact is we were created for relationships, and SM taps into that basic nature of humanity. It's true that SM provides the illusion of a relationship instead of the real thing, but I suppose that topic should be reserved for another day. SM is a powerful platform for marketing because marketing is first and foremost about relationships with our readers. Author and writing coach Shelley Hitz offered a great summary about marketing in one of her Facebook posts: "Marketing is simply forming a relationship with your target audience—getting to know them and allowing them to get to know, like, and trust you."

SM needs to become the author's best friend. Through SM, we can reach out to people and expand our connections or personal influence. In *APE: How to Publish a Book*, Guy Kawasaki and Shawn Welch wrote, "Social media provides the fastest, easiest, and cheapest way to build a platform…"[1] Because our friends and associates can share something we write, we may find our book or blog going viral through the help of a few well placed "shares."

Notice that in the Kawasaki and Welch quote I did not include the whole sentence. This sentence came from a chapter on building a platform, which is tedious work. The rest of that sentence said, "...but it requires at least an hour or two per day for six to twelve months." I don't believe you are required to invest an hour or two per day on SM, but you need to invest a regular amount.

My book, *Immovable: Standing Firm in the Last Days*, addresses circumstances the church is facing today. After hearing a news report a couple of years ago about some things going on in our country, I put *Immovable* on sale for ninety-nine cents so as many people as possible could be encouraged by my message. I did not follow an advertising campaign or pay money to have my book promoted. I put a post on Facebook and Twitter. Two days later, my book slipped into the top ten in two different categories on Amazon and made it to number four on the bestseller list in those categories. Making the bestseller list happened because of SM.

Important Social Media Principles

Here are some key principles you should keep tucked away in your mind as you venture into the deeper waters of social media marketing.

* Social media is first of all social. The purpose of SM is to connect with people. If you use your platform only to push your product, people will turn a deaf ear and a blind eye. This concept is of such importance I will address it further in this chapter.

- Remember to follow proper protocol. You should consider accepted etiquette as you tap into various SM platforms. Good etiquette addresses all types of issues. For example, you should not TYPE IN ALL CAPITAL LETTERS (which is like shouting at someone) and avoid responding to someone when you are angry. You may want to consider reading up on SM etiquette. You'll find numerous websites and books available on the topic. For example, I paid $1.99 for Jennifer Kane's book: *Social Media Etiquette for Business: 100 Ways to Communicate with Grace and Class.*[2]

- Respond to people when they reply to your post. Remember that SM is for the purpose of interacting, so don't forget to share a reply when someone honors you with a response to your post.

- Make sure your profile is complete. People may want to find out more about you and check out your other internet sources. Give others as much information as possible on your profile so they will know who you are and what your goals are on that particular platform. Include your website address in your profile so interested parties can find their way to your marketing hub.

- Remember that social media is public; anyone can read your comments. If you're a Christian, make sure you're representing Christ well to both Christians and non-Christians before the comment is posted. If it could hurt your overall mission, keep the thought to yourself or save it for the proper audience.

- Be beneficial. *Always add value to people through your social media posts.* This principle may mean sharing a link to a

website that will help others or offering a free download
of something you have written.

- If you want others to share your post, be willing to share
  their posts.
- Remember words are important. There is always more
  than one way to say something, so choose your words
  carefully. You could say, "Buy my book," but that is always a turn off. Offer a statement from your book and
  then include the Amazon link for where customers can
  download the whole digital copy.
- Use pictures or video. You may get more shares and
  more mileage out of a post if it includes an engaging picture or video. Remember to be careful about using copy-
  righted materials, but visuals have a longer life in the
  internet world than just words.

Social Media Platforms

One tech savvy entrepreneur defined a platform as "a
group of technologies that are used as a base upon which
other applications, processes, or technologies are developed."[3] Let's think of a platform as a springboard into a system of communication. Social media platforms, such as
Facebook, Twitter, and LinkedIn, have different audiences
and provide experiences in communicating thoughts and
messages to friends and associates.

- Facebook is by far the most popular social media platform with 1.62 billion people visiting it each day.[4] According to Pew Research, sixty-nine percent of adults in
  the United States use Facebook, and many do it daily,
  spending an average of up to twenty minutes on the site
  per visit.[5] Forty-six percent of senior adults in the U. S.

use this platform, and the number of seniors on Facebook has doubled since 2012.[6] Through Facebook, you can create a profile, share pictures and update your status. Your "friends" can share comments and "like" your posts. When friends "like" something that you post, their friends become privy to the fact that they liked your comments. Because Facebook is the third most visited website in the world, third only to Google and Wikipedia, authors should consider using this platform as a marketing tool.[7]

You can see how this platform can multiply your marketing impact. Your well-placed comment can go viral, with a little help from your friends. Even though your comments, or posts, on Facebook are not limited in space, you will find that your followers are not interested in reading long, drawn out comments. We live in a world that appreciates concise statements.

With over a billion people using Facebook on a regular basis, authors discover this social media platform to be essential to their marketing strategy. Paul Fairbrother suggests we spend four hours per week to manage our Facebook accounts.[8]

Facebook offers both personal pages and business pages. I have chosen to have a personal page and an author page. Through your personal page, you attract "friends" and share personal information about your life and activities. Your business or author page will draw "likes," and you can share information about your book topics and writing activities. You can share some of the same type of material on both formats, but you will want to edit it a little to keep it unique. You can visit my personal Facebook page at facebook.com/triordan8 and compare it to my author Facebook page at facebook.com/authortimriordan.

- YouTube is viewed as a video posting site more than a social media platform; however, it is very much a SM site allowing people to interact with others over posted videos. YouTube has nearly two billion users, causing it to be the second most popular SM site, with one billion hours of video viewed every day. It's the world's second largest search engine (owned by Google by the way), and eight out of ten adults, age eighteen to forty-nine, watch YouTube every month.[9] If you can create an engaging video about your book with follow-up videos about your topic, you have the potential of reaching many people with your message. I will address using videos briefly in another chapter.

- If you were putting social media in order of influence, you'd have to put Instagram next. It has about one billion users each month, and in 2018, nearly thirty-two percent of Americans used it. Instagram is a photo/video sharing site that is owned by Facebook but attracts a younger population. In our visual culture, Instagram and its rival Snapchat are growing quickly. Authors have to creatively use pictures and other graphics to engage Instagram users.

- LinkedIn has more than 610 million users and gets two new members every second.[10] This platform seems to be more of a niche networking system allowing people to network through professional relationships. It started out as a service used for posting resumes and has become the largest online professional network in the world, making it useful for authors.

Some people question the usefulness of LinkedIn for authors in regard to building a platform, but it can be useful in making professional connections. Marketing experts Jelen and McCallister urge authors to use LinkedIn because talent scouts, agents, and publishers use this service to research potential clients. It also seems that people with LinkedIn accounts get better online representation through Google searches.

- Twitter is another popular social media platform with an estimated 321,000,000 unique monthly visitors.[11] It is one of the ten most visited websites worldwide and averages almost 500 million "tweets" a day.[12] You communicate with people on Twitter by posting tweets of 280 characters or less (shorter is better—the most common is thirty-three characters), and subscribers define topics with hashtags (#99cents, #mustread, etc.). People choose to follow you, and if they happen to be tuned in, they can read your tweets.

Only people who follow you see your tweets, but if someone chooses to do so, they can "retweet" your post so all of their followers can read it. According to Statista, "Twenty-two percent of online adults currently use Twitter, and forty percent of Americans between the ages of eighteen to twenty-nine use Twitter regularly.[13] Ninety-three percent of those who choose to follow a particular small to medium-size business on Twitter plan to purchase from those they follow.[14]

Think about the significance of this fact for authors. Though you will be limited to 280 characters, Twitter can become the door through which interested parties pass to find out more information from your website, blog, or other internet sources.

- Pinterest was the fastest growing social media site in 2014, but it has been passed by Instagram. On Pinterest, people share interesting discoveries by "pinning" them to their page, and most people who frequent this site are women. Eighty-three percent of weekly users plan to make a purchase from a brand they pin on their account.[15] In order for Pinterest to be a useful marketing resource in the writing business or ministry, authors have to pull quotes from their books or create other creative visuals to point followers to their main marketing hub. Because you will have to "pin" something to the site, you may need to post a quote from your book with an engaging visual. This visual can be created with Photoshop, Canva, or another graphic arts program. By tapping into Pinterest, you are potentially connecting to 250,000,000 people.[16]

These six social media sites are part of a growing list that also includes Snapchat, Tumblr, Meetup, and a number of others. The key is to find the ones that work for you. I have shared these six because you will have the greatest success if you tie into one of the larger services.

Putting Social Back into Social Media

One of the inordinate challenges in life is to overcome a me-centered existence. Let's face it, selfishness is hardwired into every human being, including authors, pastors, and business leaders. This reason is why the Apostle Paul said, "I die daily." I said earlier that if we are going to use SM to help accomplish our writing goals, we must remember that this platform is first and foremost social.

Authors may tap into a particular platform hoping to promote their books. The temptation is to urge everyone to "Buy my book." The problem is that people did not join Facebook or Twitter to read advertisements. They joined the site to build or strengthen relationships. A post that says "Buy my book" will not be received with open arms (or mind or wallet) but will turn off a potential reader. If you follow the "promote me" method of social media, you will lose the opportunity to influence followers with the message of your book.

Authors must join SM sites to build relationships with readers. This commitment means that we should interact with people about a variety of topics. Periodically, we can insert quotes from our books and links to our blogs, but followers must be able to view you as a real person with a real life and not just an author, always hawking his or her wares.

It's funny to think that just a few years ago the words texting, instant message, and tweet didn't exist in the context they're used today. Now, these words are a part of our regular vocabulary.

Through social media, you have the opportunity to connect to the world. The challenge is to create a plan that incorporates the right methods, social media platforms, and other marketing tools to bring about your desired success. In the next chapter, we'll focus on how to develop and follow a social media strategy.

Action Points

- Do you use social media regularly? Make a list of three reasons why SM should become your "best friend" when it comes to expanding your writing influence.
- Though I do not agree with Kawasaki and Welch when they said it would take an hour or two per day to use SM effectively as a marketing tool, utilizing SM will take some time. Are you willing to invest the time needed to tap into this amazing resource?
- What etiquette tips come to your mind when you think about social media? I mentioned a few tips under "Important Social Media Principles." See if you can come up with others. Make a list of the top three tips you should remember as you engage through social media.
- Where is a good place for you to get royalty-free pictures you can use in social media? Why should you be concerned about royalty-free pictures? Go ahead and save a few sites on your favorites list that offer legal pictures you can use. You may want to consider a royalty-free website like Pixabay.com.
- Review the six social media platforms. Choose two that you plan to make your priority focus. If you are not already a member of the sites, join now.
- Imagine being on Facebook and wanting to post something from your book. In an attempt to be social and not just pushing your book, come up with three ways you can engage your friends in conversations about the topic of your book without saying, "Buy my book!"

Chapter Ten

Social Media Strategy

In the last chapter, I gave you only enough information to whet your appetite or cause you to run for the hills. If you're going to do something with the information I've provided about social media, as well as apply information you already know about this method of interaction, you must figure out practical steps that will lead to marketing success. Social media is a tool that should be understood, used effectively, and controlled. Don't ignore it just because you don't understand it, and don't be consumed and controlled by it either. Tap into it's strength.

Although social media may be one of my least favorite tasks, I have to remind myself it's one of the simplest and most cost effective means available to connect to readers. It is also one of the greatest ministry tools I have at my fingertips. Why wouldn't I utilize it often?

When you consider enlarging your platform through a social media strategy, you may at first feel overwhelmed. Don't get me wrong; using social media effectively takes work. Your writing success is worth the effort and investing in people should be our first goal. Tapping into social media's benefits will take a concerted, consistent effort.

Edie Melson is an expert in the field of social media, and I recommend you follow her and read anything she puts out about this topic. I had the privilege of sitting in several of her classes at the Blue Ridge Christian Writers' Conference, which I also recommend. She said that with consistent effort, it will take you about six weeks to get up to speed on the effective use of social media. Are you willing to invest six weeks in learning a valuable lesson that will help you become a successful author and a blessing to other people?

I roll my eyes when I think about social media and all the reasons I don't have time to use this method. Melson says that she does it in thirty minutes a day, four days a week. The key is having a few systems and methods that will make the task more tolerable and effective. I suggest you read Edie Melson's book, "Connections: Social Media and Networking Techniques for Writers," as well as other helpful resources on the topic.[1] In this chapter, I'll share a few thoughts on creating a strategy that works for you.

> *"By not tweeting, you are tweeting. You are sending a message."*

First Things First

The purpose of social media is to connect with people. It can be a great marketing resource, but that is a by-product of socially connecting with people. As authors, we are in the people business. No matter what kind of books you write, you should embrace the fact that your focus must be people and relationships with them. As you think about developing a social media strategy, you must think of social media as a tool to connect with people.

Relationships are about other people and not us. It is critical that we understand this principle. If you want people to engage with you, follow you, and enjoy reading your posts, don't be self-centered. I know that people's favorite topic is usually themselves but fight the urge to make your posts about you. Share posts that will help others. Retweet statements from others that have value and post links to websites that may be of benefit to readers. Ask questions about your friends on Facebook and follow up with people after they share a particular struggle or issue in their lives. See social media as a way to pour into others.

Jesus said, "Do unto others as you would have them do unto you." This guiding principle affects so many areas of our lives and applies to social media as well. We don't like to listen to people always talk about themselves, so don't fall into that trap of doing the same. Don't always post your great successes and tell everyone how awesome your kids are. Arrogance is always a turn off. Sharing successes is okay if most of your posts are about other people or point to helpful ideas.

> "Self-centered people have only one topic to talk about...
> THEMSELVES."
> Stef Harder

This concept doesn't mean that we never share anything about our books. The fact is we probably wrote our books so that we could help other people. You can periodically post a helpful quote from your book with a link where it can be purchased, but you may want to follow a 5:1 ratio on self-promotion: five posts that focus on others or point people to helpful ideas and resources versus one post that promotes your books or focuses on yourself.

To Do or Not to Do

For starters, if you choose "not to do" social media, you're making a HUGE mistake. The title of this section is not to present the option of ignoring all of social media but rather a suggestion of picking and choosing which social media platforms to use. Keep in mind that you cannot be effective at utilizing every social media platform that's available. I suggest picking a couple that seem to be a good fit for you. Here are a few suggestions for you to consider as you pick the platforms that best serve your needs.

- Which platform will best reach your audience? If you write for business leaders and professionals, LinkedIn might be a good place to start. If you write for a young audience, Instagram or Snapchat should be on your radar. Just like we must consider our audience as we write books, we must also consider our audience when we market. I've had authors tell me they don't use a certain social media platform because they don't like it. I understand this position because I've said the same thing. However, our first motivation must connect us to readers. If millions of prospective readers "hang out" on Twitter, why would we ignore a logical marketing resource? It may be that we have to get over our dislikes and put readers before our own preferences.

- Which platform best reflects you? Each social media platform seems to have its unique personality or at least reflect a personality. For example, Instagram is all about posting pictures. If you like to take pictures or if you are a very visual person, you may want to gravitate to Instagram. Twitter is brief and is more about sharing information. You only have access to 280 characters. Do you want to make a brief statement and point people to some other resource? Do you want to pass along helpful in-formation, sort of like a news reporter? Twitter may be for you. If you want to be able to share more inform-ation about a topic, you may prefer to tap into Facebook. Are you a project person and a visual person? Are you a woman or do you write for women? If you answered yes, you may prefer Pinterest.

You will be more effective with a platform that fits you. If you can enjoy it, you'll be more likely to use it.

- Which platform offers you the greatest resource for your objective? If you want to post longer videos, I suggest you use YouTube. If you prefer live videos, Facebook may be the best option.

- Which platform will give you the biggest bang for your buck? Obviously, social media doesn't cost you money, at least initially. I'm asking you which effort will bring the greatest return? Where do your potential readers hang out? Look at the platforms that will help you con-nect with the typical person who reads your books.

Plan Your Work; Work Your Plan

What's the plan? That's a great question and one you should commit to writing. I'm going to suggest a few princi-ples for you to follow as you put together an effective social media strategy.

- Pick two platforms and gain proficiency. I suggest that you make one of those platforms Facebook. Once you are on Facebook, learn how to set up a personal page and an author page (or business page). You can also create preference-specific ads on Facebook for prospective readers. My second choice is Twitter because of the number of purchase-ready followers you can accumulate on Twitter and because of the valuable use of hashtags you'll have at your disposal. Consider other possibilities as well but pick two and ignore the rest—for now.

- Use pictures as often as possible. Visuals capture people's attention best and offer greater recall. Studies show that creative graphics lead to more shares. It is also best to create your own graphics, which can be done easily through online programs, such as Canva (canva.com). Just upload a picture and add a few words. Your product is called a meme. Brad Smith reports that you will get thirty-seven percent more engagement with visuals on Facebook than simply using words, and articles with images get ninety-four percent more views.[2] Sign up for Canva and play around with creating a meme. It's not hard. You can also find great tutorials on the website to guide you. Now, post a relevant meme on Facebook and note how many likes and shares it receives.

- Are you willing to study your two social media choices for the next two weeks? How about four weeks? Remember that you need to become proficient with your social media platform of choice. You can find helpful resources through blogs and books that will be useful to you. I found a wonderful resource by Shayla Raquel that offers help on setting up and using a Facebook author page: shaylaraquel.com/ blog/ facebookauthorpages. Scott La Counte, offers additional help on his blog you can find online at ingramspark.com/blog/facebook-ads-for-authors-4-tips-to-optimize-ad-performanceHe also includes an online training course for using social media: ingramspark.com/social-media-course.

- Look into online resources that will help you plan your posts on Twitter. Consider a service like Hootsuite or Buffer to help you schedule and broadcast your tweets. Facebook will not work with either, so you'll have to post directly to Facebook. One advantage of a social media management tool is analytics and control. You can take a few minutes each morning or one morning a week to schedule your posts for the day or week. You can even set up your posts for a week and then go on vacation and not worry about social media.

- Always reply when people comment on your posts. Always. This practice shows that each person is valued and gives you the opportunity to interact with people, which is the purpose of social media.

- Consider shooting short videos and using them in your social media posts. Your videos don't have to be professional but make them as good as you can. Try to keep them under two minutes.

Prepare, Post, Respond

The three words in this subsection title could be a good summary strategy. When I say *prepare*, I mean to challenge you to study the platform. Here's a word of encouragement: you don't have to be an expert before you post. Remember that social media is about connecting to people, not expertise in what is written in the post. So, start connecting. Part of your preparing may come in the form of learning how to create memes or doing video edits. Another part of preparing is setting up your pages. Create an engaging and personal banner for the top of the page and think of relevant information you want to share in your profile. You may want to look at some other authors pages for examples.

Share relevant, timely, and consistent posts. It's possible to post too often and too little. Some of your activity may be simply liking someone's post or replying to something someone else said but remember to add your own unique posts two or three times a day. Look for creative ways to mention your book without saying, "Buy my book." Every now and then, share a quote from your book and add a link. Make sure these kinds of posts, however, are the exception and not the rule. Mention other people in your posts and point your followers to great resources from other authors. You may find these authors reciprocating the favor.

> *"Engage rather than sell...Work as a co-creator, not a marketer."*
> Tom C. Anderson

As you respond to people, be honest and real. Your readers want to know your heart before they want to read your words. People are far more apt to want to read a book by someone they feel they know than by someone they've never met. Social media provides the perfect platform for you to meet a lot of people in a short period.

Effective social media marketing requires a commitment. Just as you need to write every day, you also need to market every day. One important daily marketing tool involves using social media. Don't let it run your life but plan it into your life. I love how Edie Melson responds to the question when someone asks her how much time they need to spend on social networking: "Truthfully, the bare minimum."[3] Figure out your *bare minimum* and go for it.

Action Points

- Can you think of a time you saw products pushed on social media and were turned off by the approach? Whenever I said that social media is first and foremost not a marketing tool but rather a means by which you can connect with people, what was your reaction? If social media is not a marketing tool, why mention it in a book on marketing?

- Take a moment and write out a social media mission statement for your career or ministry as a writer.

- I listed four things to consider as you decide which social media platforms you'll use in your effort to influence people with your message. Based on that list and the social media options, which two of these options will you begin to use and why?

- Do you have a good program you can use to create graphics or edit pictures for memes? If not, sign up for Canva. Now, use whatever means you have to create a meme that communicates an important theme in your life. Post it on social media.

- Have you taken the time yet to look at my two Facebook pages? Do so now. Make a list of good things you see and things I should do to improve it. Now, make a list of what you plan to do to create the most effective page for your Facebook account.

- What is your "bare minimum" for using social media?

Chapter Eleven

Optimizing Amazon

I once heard someone say if you are a self-made man, you haven't made much. The fact is that if we want to succeed in life, we will find our greatest success out of synergistic relationships with other people. God made us for community, and we thrive in the context of friendships.

I want to introduce you to a friend that may become one of your best friends in the future: Amazon. While you will not play golf with this friend or attend the next conference together, you will find Amazon to be helpful in growing your writing career. I don't want to present the idea that your success hinges upon Amazon, but it *is* the largest book seller in the world.

Amazon presents an interesting and mysterious platform. If you want to get the most out of this wonderful resource, you must work hard to understand it and take advantage of its services.

More than Just a Store Front

I read about authors who refer to Amazon as a "store front," and at first, I saw it as a place to display products. My perspective limited me. Before I became an author, my view of Amazon was from the angle of a buyer. Amazon was a great place to find anything I wanted or needed.

As I began to study marketing and work on promoting my books, I gained new understanding of this marketing machine called Amazon.com. I learned that this resource was not just a place where buyers shopped, but also a place where sellers sold. I know that sounds obvious, but changing my perspective opened up new doors of opportunity. As a seller, I discovered Amazon functions in more roles than a place to display my books.

Search Engine

When people need to search for something on the internet, most start with Google. If you need to know something, anything for that matter, type a word or two in Google's search box, and you find possibly millions of websites offering information about your topic. Although Google is the most popular search engine, others are available. Alex Chris offered a list of the top ten search engines in the world, and the first three are Google, Bing, and Yahoo.[1] Sixty-four percent of searchers use Google. When people are searching for products, however, most of them start with Amazon. While 35% of shoppers start with Google, 38% of them begin searching on Amazon.[2]

> *"Failure to do Amazon SEO right will result in less traffic and fewer sales."*
> Mark Schenker

Have you ever thought about Amazon as a search engine? Understanding this aspect of Amazon will affect the keywords you choose as you set up your book and write your book descriptions. You should use keywords other people may type into the search box. I cannot overemphasize the importance of keywords.

I'm about halfway through writing a book called *How to Cultivate the Fruit of Success*. I hope to release it sometime in 2020 or early 2021. Do you see a word in that title that will be a popular word people may type into Amazon's search bar? *Success*. I suppose *cultivate* and *fruit* could be important words for farmers, but a lot of people search for resources on Amazon to help them experience success in life. I plan to do my best to market this book using every resource I have at my disposal, but I believe I will have added sales because the word *success* is in the title. You can test this theory by finding this book in 2021 on Amazon and see what sales rank Amazon gives it. I spent a whole chapter writing about keywords in my book *How to Write and Publish Books*. I suggest you review my comments there and study additional resources on the matter.

Marketer

Amazon will help you market your book. They offer at least five services that assist you in connecting to readers with your message. One is found in the suggestion of additional purchases. On the home page for any book, you find a section that begins with this line: "Customers who bought this item also bought…" If your book has sold enough to get noticed by Amazon's metrics, then you may appear on someone else's page as a recommended purchase.

In addition to promoting similar purchases, another feature included near the bottom of the page featuring your book is a section entitled "Customers who viewed this item also viewed…" This section offers one additional marketing tool where your book may possibly be displayed for potential customers who otherwise may never know you exist.

Another service comes in the form of a periodic email promotion. Again, obtaining this free service has to do with metrics and algorithms, but if your book qualifies, Amazon may include your book in an email by recommending it to potential customers.

A fourth marketing service you see on every product page is the review section. We will look at the importance of reviews later, but it is a key element to lead people to purchase your book.

Amazon also offers a service, called *Author Central,* to help readers get to know you as an author. I will cover this feature in more detail in another section, but readers will find this to be a way to discover your books, read about your background, and follow you on social media sites.

Publisher

Did you realize that Amazon offers publishing services? They are not a publisher like Thomas Nelson or Zondervan, but they do offer publishing services. In my opinion, Amazon opened the door for *the rest of us* to get published. Amazon's publishing service is called Kindle Direct Publishing, or KDP. When I began to write and publish, Amazon also offered a service called Createspace that was used to publish paperback books, but this service merged with KDP. For writers who can't get the attention of a major publisher or who prefer to publish on their own, Amazon offers a service to take their completed manuscript from the computer to the online bookstore. For more information on this service, visit, visit kdp.amazon.com.

KDP is not the only publishing service for self-published authors, but it is certainly one you should consider.

Social Media Platform

Although Amazon is not the same type of platform as Facebook or Instagram, it does provide a means by which people interact with one another. In defining social media, tech specialist and author Margaret Rouse said, "Social media is the collective of online communications channels dedicated to community-based input, interaction, content-sharing and collaboration."[3] Because Amazon offers community-based input, a platform for interaction between readers and authors, content-sharing, and collaboration, they are by definition a social media platform.

Allow Me to Introduce Myself

I'm sure that Amazon's bottom line is profit, and Amazon executives know that their profit increases when authors are a success. One helpful service I mentioned in the previous section is Amazon's Author Central, which allows authors to introduce themselves and their writing to potential readers.

I've often said there's no such thing as a free lunch, but in this case, Author Central is totally free. The amazing thing to me is some authors do not take advantage of this service. Let's consider some of the great features of Author Central.

You may want to get online while you're reading this section. Go to Amazon.com and type in my name (Tim

Riordan) in the search bar. One thing you'll notice right away is a number of books that I did *not* write are displayed. This annoying fact is because of either some similarity to my name or writing (Rick Riordan for example), something in the Amazon algorithm that connects it to my book, or paid advertising that connects it to my name or genre. You will have to scroll down to find all of my books.

Notice my first book in the list under my name. Regardless of which book pops up first, you will see that my name is highlighted in blue, indicating it offers a hyperlink to my Author Central page. Click on my name to explore my author page.

The first thing you will see on my author page is my picture and a list of my books for sale on Amazon. Because my novels are published under a pen name, you will have to go to Judah Knight's author page to learn about my novels.

Down the left side of the page, you'll find my bio, which introduces me to my readers. Beneath the graphics representing each of my books, you'll discover a section called "Author Updates." This section connects you to my website and the updates of my blog.

Getting the Biggest Bang

In order to optimize Amazon for your benefit, you will need to set up your book's sales page carefully. This process first means writing a great book and introducing it through your book description. I'm amazed at how little attention some authors give to their book descriptions. Work hard on this piece of copy. Get input from other authors and marketing professionals. You may even want to hire someone to write it for you.

You will also maximize the Amazon experience by using keywords in setting up your book. When you publish your book, you choose up to seven key words as a description, and these words will connect people to your book through searches. You can also use these words in your description and book title. I know I seem fixated on the topic of keywords, but this is an important marketing tool.

Another important feature offered by Amazon on your book sales page is the "Look Inside" offer. This feature offers readers the opportunity to read a portion of your book for free. Prospective readers will see this offer to the left of your book's description, and buyers can check out the opening pages of your book. Think long and hard about what you want people to read. I have started putting the dedication page of my digital books in the back of the book. Because only a certain percentage of your book shows up in the "Look Inside" offer, you don't want to waste this service on something that will not help sell your book. I like the fact my book may be dedicated to my awesome wife or amazing children, but no one else cares.

> "Content is King but engagement is Queen, and the lady rules the house."
> Mari Smith

If you publish through KDP and opt into their Kindle Select program, giveaways can also come in the form of a special promotion where you actually give your book away for free for a day or two or more. Some authors use this strategy to build readership and get reviews. I personally think it's best not to give your book away but to drop the price to ninety-nine cents as a "Countdown Deal." One reason I think it's better not to give your book away for free is giveaways do not help your sales ranking. One of your goals is to improve your Amazon algorithms, which are affected by sales ranking. You run these promotions once every ninety days, and the promotion lasts for about a week.

Reviews are another feature on your sales page that will help you sell books. It seems this issue may be one over which you have no control, but in fact, you can control it, somewhat. Obviously, readers will buy your book, and some of them will post reviews. You can't control that process. You can, however, get more reviews posted on your site. I hope you'll review the information in the next chapter to see how you can get more reviews.

Action Points

- I mentioned that Amazon is more than just a store front by sharing four additional services Amazon provides. Which of the four was most surprising to you?
- Go on Amazon and perform a search. Experiment with several words. For example, type in my name (Tim Riordan) and see several of my books pop on the list. Search the genre that best describes your book. Scan down to the sales rank number on your page (included in the personal information about your book) and write the overall Amazon bestsellers rank. Now, go to the number one book in your category. Look at the sales rank number of that book and write it down. Look at the second book. What is the sales rank? You can see you can determine a general number of your books that will need to be sold in order for you to become a bestseller in your

category. It's best to choose a genre for your book where you can become a #1 bestseller by selling fewer books. It may be a good idea to keep up with your sales rank and make note of the things you're doing to improve your overall rank.

- Set up an author page on authorcentral.amazon.com. If you haven't written a book yet, you may need to create the pieces that will go on your site once your book is published. Work hard to create the perfect page that will represent you well.

- How will you work with your Amazon sales page to get the best response?

Chapter Twelve

Getting Reviews

Reviews are important but also hard to get. Part of the reason I feel that way is because I do not like asking people to write a review for one of my books. I feel like I'm imposing upon their time, and I think many do not want to do it.

I never wrote a review until I became a published author. I now realize how crucial reviews are, so I try to bless other authors and sellers with a helpful review, assuming the book is worthy. I have had occasions when I would have given a bad review. In those cases, I chose to contact those authors and give them my review so as not to hurt their sales with a review that lasts forever. My hope has been that these authors will listen to my constructive criticism and make the needed changes.

Why Reviews?

Why reviews? Maybe that's a dumb question. Reviews are important because they present opinions readers should consider as they decide whether or not to buy your book. They also become mini advertisements as they tell customers what to expect out of your book if they choose to buy it. Reviews validate good books and weed out bad ones.

Reviews come in two forms. One type of review comes from a professional reviewing company and the other from consumers. You can pay for reviews through companies like Chanticleer (chantireviews. com), Kirkus (kirkus reviews. com/indie-reviews) or Readers' Favorite (readers favorite.

com/ref/15388). Amazon will not allow these reviews to be posted under the "Reviews" section of your sales page, but reviews can be placed under the "Editorial" section of your sales page or used sparingly in your book description. These types of reviews will help your books gain additional exposure and credibility.

Consumer reviews are a big variable, but essential. The more reviews you have the better, and your reviews should also be current. If the last review you received is two years old, it looks as if you've sold no books in a long time. Gaining reviews should be a continued focus of authors, and it requires an ongoing strategy. I'll mention a few ideas on how you can garner more consumer reviews.

Bad Reviews

Not all reviews are equal. I have learned some people write reviews out of the context of their dysfunction. Maybe that terminology sounds harsh, but I've had people give me bad reviews for the craziest reasons. I've seen this reaction in my fiction. I got a one star once because I said the Bahamas were in the Caribbean. I suppose that the Bahamas aren't the Caribbean. I saw something on a cruise website about cruising the Caribbean, and the ship went to the Bahamas. I think because that reviewer knew the boundaries of the Caribbean and I didn't, she felt inclined to be vocal about her knowledge by giving me a one star. Maybe the fact that I didn't understand the Caribbean boundaries ruined the book for this reader. I suppose that can happen.

I'm convinced some people gave my novel a one or two star because they got it for free, and the story didn't really come to a solid conclusion until the end of the second book.

If they wanted to know what happens in the story, they would have to pay for the next one. Am I cynical? Maybe. I have noticed the only time I have gotten bad reviews is when I give a book away for free. Interesting. You may want to keep that thought in mind as you decide whether or not you utilize KDP's free book promotion.

The fact is you are going to get some bad reviews. Even the Bible has a one-star review on Amazon. You will deserve some of them (God didn't, but we mortals do). Bad reviews are not all bad. In some ways, they validate your other reviews. Sarah Bolme pointed out in *Your Guide to Marketing Christian Books,* "Marketing studies show that when consumers find negative reviews sprinkled among the reviews that are positive about a product, they're more confident that the good reviews are trustworthy."[1]

> "To avoid criticism, do nothing, say nothing, and be nothing."
> Elbert Hubbard

Bad reviews can be great teachers. Before you write your negative reviewer off as deranged, consider the criticism. The reviewer may be doing you a great service. When I first published *The Long Way Home* under my pen name Judah Knight, it was twice as long and filled with mistakes. Though I maintained an average of over four stars, I had rough criticisms. Some of them were 100% right. Thanks to the negative reviews, I went back and corrected my mistakes. I rewrote the book, turned it into two books, republished them, and have had good success.

Don't lose sleep over bad reviews. We all want to be validated and appreciated, but not everyone will love our books. It's okay. Do your best. Learn from mistakes. If you respond to a reviewer, be nice. Don't try to correct a reviewer or defend yourself. I recently opted not to stay in an Airbnb house because the owner blasted a person for writing a negative review. If the negative review is not deserved, it will be covered over by a ton of positive reviews.

How to Get Reviews

Because reviews are essential, how do you get them? My first answer is simple and the most effective. Ask for them. I always feel awkward asking for reviews, but I've come to realize that my future success depends in part on a consistent flow of good reviews. When I mention this approach, the first thing that probably comes to your mind is asking your friends and family members to read your book and write a review. That option is certainly one thing we can do but consider additional ways from the list below.

- Contact beta readers to read your manuscript before you publish it and be prepared to post a review as soon as it's published. This method will probably include friends and family members, but you can expand that circle to include more readers. Amazon prefers reviews from readers other than our relatives. When enlisting beta readers, authors will send them an "Advanced Review Copy" (ARC) of their books. You can send your book as a pdf file, so it doesn't cost you anything. These readers (as well as anyone who receives a free copy of your book as a swap for a review) should include in their review they were given a free advance copy of the book

for their honest review. You may want to offer guidelines on how to leave a review on Amazon. Wikihow offers step-by-step help: wikihow.com/Leave-a-Review-
on-Amazon.

- Get help from your street team. I'll write about your
street team in the chapter on launching your book, but
basically, it's a group of people who are willing to help
you promote your book. This group could be considered
a part of the beta reader group, but they will also represent people who believe in you and your message. You
should be prepared to send them a pdf copy of your
book as well.

- Include a request for a review in the front and back of
your book. I include the request in the front of my book
because readers can have that on their minds as they
begin my book. The request in the back becomes a reminder of something they've already considered. I have
discovered many people read my books, and I assume
they read my request for a review, but still choose not to
write one.

- Contact Amazon reviewers. You'll discover ready reviewers from reading reviews of similar books in your
genre. You can find the profile for some reviewers by
clicking on their name in a review. For example, if you
read one of my reviews, you'll see my website (tim
riordan.com) is included on my profile. You'd be able to
contact me through my website. Sometimes, reviewers
may offer to purchase a copy of your book instead of
receiving an ARC. I typically buy my own copy when
reviewing someone else's book. I know the value of the

words "verified purchase" that's added to my review, and I don't mind buying a book that's going to help me as well as help them. Amazon also posts their top reviewers at amazon.com/review/top-reviewers/ref=cm _cr_tr_link_1.

- Ask for a review from your email subscribers. I'll cover email marketing in the next chapter, but it's okay to ask for reviews when you correspond with your readers. Don't ask often because your email readers don't want to feel used. I'll address the importance of making subscribers feel valued in another chapter.

- You can reach out to readers in reading clubs, writing groups, and organizations. Authors are readers. Join author groups, and if it's acceptable, promote your book from time to time. Authors may be more likely to leave a review.

- Join a review service. You can find services online where you pay to join, and they promote your book to readers who are willing to write reviews. Readers are willing to join a group because they love to read and know that they will receive free books if they're willing to be a part of the group. This practice is acceptable on Amazon because you're not paying for a review. You're paying to join a marketing service. Reviewers through these services are not paid for reviews they write.

- Request reviews from book bloggers. I've had success with this approach. You'll find people who write blogs about books and are willing to post your review on Amazon or Goodreads. They may post reviews because they love books. It's possible they've monetized their blogs through advertising or another way. The more books they review, the more traffic they drive to their site, which in turn makes them more money. The advantage for authors is that we get good, honest reviews.

- Book giveaways are another way to get reviews. I mentioned in another place that when I offer a free giveaway through Amazon's free book promotion for a period, I have a greater possibility of getting negative reviews. A good option is Goodreads giveaway program, though they charge a fee. You don't have guarantees of reviews, but I've found Goodreads winners seem more aware of the value of reviews.

> *"Bad reviews can simply mean the wrong person is reading your book."*
> Paul Youlten

- Join Author Marketing Club (currently costs $97) and get access to their resources, including a "Review Grabber Tool." This tool simplifies the process of finding reviewers on Amazon and offers you a download of prospective reviewers.

What's Next?

Once you receive reviews, it's a good idea to thank the reviewers. If you know how to contact them, send them an email. It may require a message on Facebook or Twitter. You can enter a comment sometimes on the retail site (like Amazon). Remember to stay positive. Don't justify yourself or correct the reviewers. Just thank them for taking the time to share their opinions.

Don't become satisfied or complacent. Writing this paragraph reminds me I have to get back to seeking out reviewers for my books. I'm sure someone knows a statistic on how many book sales it takes to generate one review, but I can tell you the number is high. Maybe it's different for every author, but I sell a lot of books before someone leaves a review. This fact means if I don't work at getting reviews, I will be lacking in this crucial key to marketing success.

As you consider a strategy for marketing, you must make sure steps that will bring about consistent reviews are on the list. I hope you'll see your review numbers growing, and you can be sure the more reviews you have, the better. Look for ways to tie gaining reviews to other marketing steps.

I challenge you to work hard at getting as many reviews as possible during the first few months your book is released. I've not made this effort in the past, but it's my new challenge. I used to strive to get ten reviews during the first month, but that number is not enough. My problem is I'm busy with other activities, or I start focusing too quickly on my next book. Take time to market and work hard to get more reviews.

Action Points
- Make a list of ten good reasons you should work hard to get book reviews.
- Take a few minutes to review the three review sites I mentioned in the early part of this chapter (Kirkus, Chanticleer, and Readers Favorite). What are advantages and disadvantages of each site? Google other review services and add them to your list.

- Brainstorm a list of reasons bad reviews can be good. Create a process you'll follow when you get a bad review to turn it into something positive.
- Review the list of ways to get consumer reviews. What methods will you make an active part of your marketing strategy? What specific steps will you implement now?
- Find a list of book bloggers by performing a Google search or through searching Facebook. Create a list of these sites and save it for future reference.
- Make a list of ten people you know whom you could ask to become a beta reader. Contact them and see if they'd be willing to help you out.

Chapter Thirteen
Email Marketing

Although every successful author I know would admonish us not to put our eggs into one basket, they would also urge us to create an email marketing list. I have heard and read numerous times that regardless of what you add to your marketing strategy, this list is one tool every author should include. Author and marketing expert Rob Eagar said, "There is no better way to ensure future success than growing a large email list."[1]

You have probably signed up for an email newsletter. Someone offers you a free book or recipe or another resource. You have to put in your name and an email address, and this person or company sends you whatever he or she is offering. You you get a gift, and they received your email address. Unless you choose to opt out, you will receive emails from this person or company in the future.

Here's a general description of email marketing. A person goes to an author's website, and after ten seconds, an offer for a free book pops up. The reader enters his or her name and email address to receive the gift. The author begins a relationship with the reader by sending a meaningful email to the reader once a week. Authors may share insight, point readers to other relevant internet material, offer additional free resources, share personal stories, and announce new book releases. Theoretically, if people give me permission to send them an email, they are likely to open my correspondence. When I announce a new book release, I have a list of ready buyers seeing my announcement.

Does Email Marketing Work?

First of all, it's important to define what "work" means. If you want to know if email marketing makes you thousands of dollars, my answer is "that depends." However, if you want to know if email marketing will help you accomplish your mission of influencing other people with your writing, I'd say, "Definitely yes." There is nothing wrong with making a living from your writing, and email marketing will be an important piece of your strategy that helps accomplish that kind of goal. I've mentioned before money shouldn't be the first thing on our minds. Our first priority is not to make a living but to make a difference. Will email marketing help make a difference? Yes. On top of that, it can also help us have financial success if we use it correctly.

Some people question whether or not email marketing can still be viable. Caroline Forsey shared interesting statistics regarding email marketing, and one of those statistics said ninety-nine percent of consumers check their email every day.[2] According to Forsey, I'd say you have a good shot at someone seeing your email. Here are more interesting statistics related to email marketing:

- According to Statista, in 2017, there were 3.7 billion email users, and this number is expected to grow to 4.23 billion by 2022.[3]
- According to *Campaign Monitor*, only six percent of your Facebook followers or fans will see a particular post, whereas emails sent out through a marketing campaign have a twenty to thirty percent open rate.[4] Christian

romance writer Hallee Bridgeman told a group attending her seminar at the Blue Ridge Christian Writers' Conference she has an astounding eighty-one percent open rate.

- *Campaign Monitor* also pointed out that click through rates from emails are around three percent while click-throughs on Tweets are around 0.5%. This statistic means you are six times more likely to get a click-through from an email campaign than you are from a tweet.[5]
- *MarketingSherpa* revealed the results of an important survey: "Seventy-two percent of people prefer to receive promotional content through email, compared to seventeen percent who prefer social media."[6]
- A few years ago, McKinsey Consulting pointed out email is forty times more effective at acquiring customers than Facebook and Twitter combined.[7]

Does email marketing work? The obvious answer is yes, but why? One reason it has a great track record is most people still open up email every day. Another is you can send emails only to people who have first given you permission. In a sense, you have been invited into their inbox. Email is also FREE! Gone are the days where you would have to spend thousands of dollars to send out an advertising piece to a certain zip code or collection of addresses.

A successful email marketing strategy consists of several key steps or components. First of all, you have to gather email addresses of potential customers. Secondly, you'll need to send out regular emails that your potential customers will want to open and read. Thirdly, you'll need to turn your regular email readers into ready book buyers. Sounds simple, right? Let's look in more detail at the process.

Gathering Emails

How do you get emails? There's only one way. Ask for them. It's easy to ask your friends and acquaintances for their email addresses. We do it all the time. The challenge is finding a way to ask for the email addresses of people you've never met.

If you are a public speaker, one easy way to do it is invite listeners to sign up for your email newsletter. You could have a card in every seat that listeners could complete, or they could stop by your book table. You could even offer a drawing from the stack of cards turned in and give a prize to the winner.

Public speaking is a wonderful marketing tool that offers opportunities for influence and book sales, and I'll cover this method in a later chapter. What if you can't do a lot of public speaking right now or no one wants you to speak at his or her event? There's got to be a better way to get email addresses. I've got good news: there is.

The Offer

One of the best ways to get an email address from someone you've never met is offer a swap. We do this all the time. Think about the last time you bought something from a yard sale or from the want ads section of a newspaper. I bought a dishwasher after reading an ad on Craigslist. I had never met the woman before, but I gave her seventy-five dollars, and she gave me the appliance. It was a swap. I gave her something of value she wanted, money, for something of value I wanted, a dishwasher.

Obtaining email addresses from prospective buyers is no different. In this case, you're probably not going to offer them money for their addresses. You will, however, offer them something of value that some experts refer to as a *lead magnet*. You may call it a free gift, but in fact, it's not free—even to them. It will cost them their email addresses. It will also cost you something—time.

> "Email marketing is still going strong today and is possibly the best possible strategy for your business."
> Neil Patel

The offer has to be something you can generate and something your reader will want. Author and entrepreneur Matthew Paulson wrote in his book *Email Marketing Demystified*, "A good lead magnet will help your website visitors learn a specific skill, solve a specific problem, or accomplish a specific task."[8] In our case as authors, the "something" we generate is a book or other written resource we can offer as a pdf. At the same time, this will be something a reader will be interested in receiving.

For my lead magnet, I offer a book I wrote on how to read the Psalms. I wrote a book on Psalms called *Songs from the Heart: Meeting with God in the Psalms*. I decided to go another step and create a teaching guide on how to read and study the Psalms. If I had this book published as a paperback and mailed it to readers, my cost would be around six dollars per book. That proposition would get expensive. The best option is offer a written resource as a pdf file which people can download onto their computers.

You must remember people will be giving you their email address and access to their inbox. Don't be cheap. Make sure your offer is really worth getting. My offer is a legitimate book that took time and effort to write and publish. I did the research, wrote the book, paid for the editing, involved multiple readers, and got help with graphics. I could sell this digital book for $2.99 or more, but I give it away. For one thing, I'm grateful for the privilege to influence people with my writing. From another perspective, I get email addresses and establish long-term relationships with new readers.

I'll say more about the quality of your offer, but make sure your offer is a real win for readers. If your offer ends up being a cheap two-page list anyone can find on the internet, people will feel cheated and opt out of your newsletter. On the other hand, if you give them a gift that raises their eyebrows, you may have just made a long-term connection.

The Mechanism

You may be nodding your head in agreement when you think about the process of writing as a valuable resource for which readers will be grateful. After all, writing is what we do. Your real question may have to do with how you'll go about putting this offer in front of people to bring results. I'm glad you asked.

To accomplish this task, you'll have to enlist the help of an email marketing service, and you'll be required to launch your offer to readers from a platform that has their attention.

You'll find a number of email services available, and the platform is usually an author's website and social media. Chapter Eight covers a lot of information about building a website, and Chapters Nine and Ten introduce social media platforms. Let's focus our attention on locating the proper email marketing service.

When I say, "email marketing service," I'm referring to a company that can help you get someone's email, create an address book that is accessible to you, and be able to generate emails to your list at a later date. If you Google the top email marketing services, you'll find different companies offering services. Hostingfacts.com offers a current list of what they determined to be the top ten services along with descriptions of each service:

- Constant Contact
- SendInBlue
- MailChimp
- ConvertKit
- Drip
- AWeber
- Mailerlite
- ActiveCampaign[9]

My church uses Constant Contact, and I currently use a service called TrafficWave.

Cost is an important factor, but you should consider other issues as well. Your email service should provide a way to receive people's email addresses, offer an automated email program for on-boarding new subscribers, assist you in creating professional looking emails, offer an easy method for subscribers to opt out, and provide processes by which you can satisfy legal guidelines and display good internet etiquette. Most email companies offer these services.

When you sign up for my newsletter (and receive a gift), you will receive an automatic email one day later thanking you for signing up and for requesting my free book. Five

> "Authors who sell a lot of books directly to their fans use email marketing as their sales weapon of choice."
> Rob Eagar

days later, you'll receive another automatic email that introduces me. Seven days after that, I send out a short email that introduces the reader to my book on Psalms with some of the background information. After that, you'll receive emails on each of my nonfiction books. I do not always ask for reviews or ask readers to purchase my books, and sometimes, I offer portions of one of my books for free.

In addition to automated emails, I also use the email broadcasting service. I periodically write an email that I send to subscribers. This email includes a newsletter and various updates about my writing. I also use this broadcast feature to create intentional marketing communications on a particular book. Experts tell you to communicate with people on your email list around once per week. This decision is yours to make, but you should stay in touch so your readers will know who you are. Once a month is not enough.

The Secret to Email Marketing Success

The secret to success with an email marketing strategy is open rate. There's no benefit to having 2000 subscribers if only ten of them open your emails. Once people have given you permission to write to them by giving you their email addresses, your greatest success comes when your readers anticipate your emails. This expectation comes after you have proven your emails are worth reading. If an author sends only emails that urge readers to purchase their books, those readers will stop opening the emails and may opt out of receiving them. If the emails offer worthwhile material, fun contests, useful resources, and the occasional book promotion, you'll have a growing, ready audience.

According to CampaignMonitor.com, the average open rate for emails sent out through email marketing is 17.92%.[10] You may think that doesn't seem high, but less than ten percent of your Facebook followers will see your post, so in comparison, nearly eighteen percent is not too bad. If you make sure your content is worth opening and your subscribers feel connected to you because of your consistent and meaningful posts, your open rate will increase. It's possible to have a twenty-five percent, thirty-five percent, or even fifty percent open rate.

I suggest you keep records of open rates and compare them with previous emails. Work hard to increase the open rate. If you've fallen below the average, evaluate your practices and create an improvement strategy you'll follow.

Action Points

- Have you taken email marketing seriously? After reading this chapter, how important do you think email marketing will be to your overall marketing strategy?
- Do you have an email marketing service? Review the websites for the services I mentioned and compare them. Which service do you prefer to use? Go ahead and sign up for it. Find tutorials on using this service and

spend some time getting familiar with how to launch a newsletter. Most companies offer training videos.

- Write out an email marketing strategy or plan. Include two or three automated onboarding notes your subscribers will receive.

- What lead magnet will you offer? Is it completed? If not, when will you have it ready to offer as a free gift? You may need to spend some time learning how to create a landing page for your free offer. Your email marketing service should offer a tutorial for that purpose.

- Make a list of five ways you're going to ensure your emails will have a higher open rate than 17.92%.

Chapter Fourteen

Video Marketing

If a picture is worth a thousand words, how many words is a video worth? The answer has to be some exponential number you can't imagine. I remember a few years ago everyone was talking about how important it was to add photos to every post. Marketing experts tell us video is the new language of consumers. The world is changing so quickly it's difficult to get accurate statistics, but here are a few to get you thinking (even if by the time you read them, they are out of date):

- In 2016, video accounted for seventy-three percent of internet traffic.
- Cisco Systems predicts by 2021, video will constitute eighty-two percent of internet traffic.[1]
- Live video is expected to see the greatest growth in the near future.
- According to *Tubular Insights*, sixty-four percent of consumers will make a purchase after watching a video on a social platform.[2]
- On average, people spend 2.6 times more time on webpages with video than on those without it.[3]
- David Hayes says eighty-seven percent of businesses use video for marketing.[4]
- In 2017, people watched over one billion hours of video daily on YouTube.

It should be clear video is here to stay, and video marketing is the new weapon of entrepreneurs and successful authors. The challenge is for authors to learn how to tap into this incredible resource and use it to accomplish their mission. Video marketing is complex and exciting. It will take much more than a chapter in this book to guide readers to tap into all its potential, but we'll use this chapter as an introduction to this wonderful resource. In these short pages, we'll consider the purpose, process, possibilities, and plans for video marketing. I hope to expand upon this topic in future writings.

The Purpose of Video Marketing

I could answer the question of the purpose of video marketing with one quick statement: to sell more books. This answer is not only inadequate, but it is also wrong. Ultimately, the purpose of video marketing is to assist in accomplishing the mission of the marketer. What is your mission as an author? Let's look at how video marketing can help.

It's obvious that video is a wonderful tool for selling products. Businesses are using it all over the globe. The statistics I shared earlier are a testament to that reality. If your objective is to sell more books to make more money, I'd suggest you better use video to help accomplish that goal. If your mission is to connect with readers and inspire them, video is an essential tool in your toolbox.

Video helps us to connect better to our readers. Remember, marketing is a relationship between a seller and a buyer. As authors, our mission is to connect with our readers and build trust. As our readers come to understand we have their best interests at heart, they will read our words and allow us to influence their lives. Even through fiction, we can still influence readers to do the right thing and to become the right people. Video is the best marketing medium to accomplish this purpose.

Think about the social aspect of video. We call Twitter "social media," but 140 or 280 characters are not very social. When you add video to that media, however, readers see you as you are. They hear your heart and connect with the real you. It's true that you can still hide in front of a camera; actors and actresses do it all the time. However, if you want to connect with your readers, video is one of the fastest and easiest ways to make that connection. Through video, readers see your expressions and encounter your feelings and passions. They will feel more personally connected.

Video touches the heart more quickly than any other medium. Video combines the power of words, the emotion of music, and the imagination of visual art to touch people in the deepest places of their souls. I can deliver a piece of copy to your inbox that invites you to consider the powerful teaching of Psalm 23, but that wouldn't compare to a video that

> *"As an online entrepreneur, video marketing is your single most powerful tool for getting more visibility."*
> Lou Bortone

combines moving music with persuasive words and engaging scenery of a shepherd caring for his sheep in the lush, green countryside. One reason book trailers have become so effective is they connect to the emotions of readers better than any other form of marketing. These trailers need to be done well for that happen, but nevertheless, they have the potential for a huge impact upon readers.

Video enables us to expand our topics. Writers can use video to pick up where the books leave off. This additional expression can come in the form of video newsletters or supplementary teaching that takes your reader to the next level on the topic covered in your book. Video provides you the opportunity to teach or illustrate with visuals and creative teaching techniques that could never be utilized on the written page.

The Process of Video Marketing

I've included a section on planning your video, but before you press the record button on your smart phone, spend serious time planning your video marketing strategy and content for the video. For video to be effective in marketing, you must use it on a regular basis. You can't just post a video book trailer and pack up your video camera until you complete your next book. Video is too powerful not to use on a regular basis. In my concluding thoughts of this book, I'll challenge you to figure out your marketing strategy. Make sure video is a part of that plan.

> *"Each video you make is like a free workforce with the added bonus of working for you 24/7."*
> Ben Simon

What's the proper length? Once you've put together an effective plan, you'll need to figure out how to shoot a video and prepare its use. One important principle to follow is the axiom that *less is more*. If you are a preacher, like me, you may find this task a bit daunting. I jokingly say I can't say my name in ten minutes. A seminary professor once said that if you haven't struck oil after twenty minutes, quit boring.

The average length for videos in the video marketing realm is about four minutes. You must consider; however, this number includes video training that's connected to marketing. If you remove those videos, you'll find most effective videos are around two minutes or less. Remember people's attention spans have grown shorter.

I read an article that stated the average attention span has dropped from twelve seconds to eight seconds. According to the article, our attention spans are less than the nine-second attention span of a goldfish. I've uncovered additional evidence those numbers may not be correct. Regardless of the exact number, our society does not seem to be strengthening the attention spans of people.

Years ago, television commercials luxuriated in thirty-second video pitches, but today, advertisers realize they need to shorten the presentation to fifteen seconds. Researchers learned nearly a fifth of viewers clicked out of a video in the first ten seconds. We also learned videos hold our attention longer than words in an ad or photograph. It may be hard to promote your book in ten seconds, but these facts should discourage us from droning on in a boring presentation. As you plan your video, think short. Think less than two minutes or you may lose them.

What's the proper approach? The good news is there's no one way to make a great video. You may find a few key principles, however, will help you create an effective video. As with all marketing, we must show how we can meet the needs of prospective readers. Our verbiage should focus on "you" (them) and not us. Speak straight to your audience.

Consider the power of a story. Stories sell. Watch commercials and notice how often stories are used to sell a product. Your focus could be the story of someone who was helped by your book. People read book reviews, so why not include testimonials in a video? You could use a story to relate the purpose of your book. I've used the story of my professor quoting Psalms in a bomb shelter during World War II to relate the power of the Psalms. I think that idea is an engaging way to invite people to use my book, *Songs from the Heart: Meeting God in the Psalms*, as a resource to help them experience the same power of God.

> "Stories are one of the most powerful tools you can use to engage and connect with your audience."
> Tony Robbins

Remember people are selfish. An important marketing principle is people want to know what's in it for them. I mentioned in an earlier chapter our marketing methods should always first address what readers will get out of reading our books. We should try to use video to address certain needs in the lives of readers and show how our books can help meet those needs.

Consider how this truth affects one of the most basic and effective uses of videos for any entrepreneur: the introduction video. When someone goes to your website, it's helpful to have a short welcome video included on the homepage, but also include an introduction video. It's a short biographical video about yourself. Remember that even though an introduction video should introduce you to your prospective reader, you have to do so by revealing how your books will meet a certain need in your readers' lives. Most people are more focused on themselves.

As a novelist, writing about romance, action, and adventure, I try to move quickly to the fact I want to help readers experience the kind of relationships they've dreamed of having. As a non-fiction writer, I want to introduce myself in a way as to convey I want to help readers experience a passionate and meaningful relationship with Jesus Christ.

> "If you truly want to connect with your target audience, you need to share yourself with them on a regular basis."
> Jon James

But how do I make a video? When we think of process, we think we need specific instructions on how to create a video for marketing purposes. The actual process is simple. You shoot the video, edit for whatever medium you plan to use, and upload it. That sounds easier than it is. I plan my video first to reduce the number of takes, and by doing so, I trim editing time. We live in an age when raw video footage is acceptable. People are not looking for the perfect take. There's a place for recording a selfie on video and posting it in your social media feed. At other times, you'll need to up-load your video to editing software and tweak it.

I'll have to cover equipment and techniques another time, but you can start with minimal equipment. If you have a smart phone, you've got a great start. I suggest you also invest in a cheap lapel microphone you can plug into your phone and a small tripod to hold your phone. Start some-where, start small, use your videos as soon as possible, and improve as you go along.

What are the Possibilities of Video Marketing?

The possibilities are only limited by your creativity and possibly your budget. Realizing you may come up with additional ideas, let's at least divide the possibilities into on-camera and off-camera formats as well as promotional, instructive, and on mission videos.

In on-camera videos, you are actually "on-camera." You are in the video. You create an on-camera video by looking into the camera and talking about the topic of your book. You can also interview other professionals in the field of your book's topic. On-camera video would include live video feed on social media. Live video is growing in popularity. You can "go live" on social media or interact with people through a webinar.

In off-camera videos, you're not in the video. You can do this video with pictures and a voice-over. You could also video other people telling a story or acting out a story line. You'll find a lot of low-end book trailers that contain only pictures, music, and printed script for the viewer to read.

A word of caution; don't be hokey. I think you understand what I mean. Don't be corny, tacky, or cheesy. Do your best to present as professional a video as possible. I suggest you don't just use your own opinion and expertise to determine whether or not something is appropriate. Also, don't surround yourself with "yes people." For example, your mother may always think what you do is wonderful.

I've seen bad book trailers and wondered why someone didn't stop the creators from posting it before they hurt their sales. Use video but use it well. This goal may mean you stay away from video drama if you can't do it with excellence.

How do you Plan for Video Marketing?

Plan your video. Script out what you want to say. Your video should be as conversational, real, and authentic. Try to avoid reading your script or following a teleprompter. Viewers can usually tell when someone is reading. It may help you to write out what you want to say so you will have considered the content up front. If you're interviewing someone, you should discuss the video with the other per-son before pressing *record*.

You need to plan your video marketing strategy. How often will you use video? How can you enhance your website with video? On which social media platforms do you plan to utilize video? Will you offer a regular video on your blog or will you ever use a live video feed on Facebook? How will you use book trailers with your book launches? What else can you do during launches with a video to keep the newness of your book in front of people? Write out your plan. Use a calendar. Try to work video presentations into your overall marketing plan.

Regarding your website, consider using a welcome video and an introduction video. The welcome video will be a short welcome and overview of your website. Express your purpose statement. Remember the viewer is going to give you a short time, so tell them why you're going to help them accomplish their dreams or, at least, what's in it for them.

Your introduction video can include short stories from your past and what motivated you to write in the first place. Share about your passions, hobbies, and family.

I know I have only touched the surface of this marketing method, but what I have given you is, at least, enough to whet your appetite. I hope you'll watch for my next book on video marketing and additional resources I'll offer along the way. In the meantime, pull out a pen and piece of paper and develop a plan to use video. Write out a script, pull out your smart phone, and press record.

> "Video content impacts organic performance more than any other asset that can be displayed on a web page."
> Tanu Javeri

Action Points

- Review the statistics I provided about video marketing. What's your reaction to these facts? Google the words "video marketing statistics" and read additional facts about this powerful medium. Is there any reason you shouldn't learn how to utilize this important tool?
- Review your purpose statement for writing. Now, write out a statement of purpose for using video as a part of your marketing strategy. Make a list of reasons why you should employ video in your overall strategy.
- Remember people are basically selfish. Now, brainstorm what you might say on a video to introduce yourself and how your book will meet the needs of your reader. Remember to say "you" and offer practical help.

- What are some ways you can use video marketing? Can you make a book trailer? Could you have someone interview you about your book? Is there some additional teaching you can put on video that will increase your chances of being found by a Google search?
- Visit Fiverr.com and review the services offered for creating video book trailers.
- Go ahead and shoot a welcome video for your website. You may trash it and do it again later but make one now for practice. Compose a script and give it a shot. Once you've filmed a welcome video, shoot another one to introduce yourself to readers.

Chapter Fifteen

Preparation for Face-to-Face Encounters

I mentioned earlier in this book that marketing is a relationship formed between the seller and buyer. Can you think of a better way to form a relationship than meeting face-to-face? In this technologically driven society, people are moving farther and farther apart. Conversations have become limited to less than 300 characters, and many people have succumbed to dishonesty in an attempt to make their lives more interesting. Connecting with readers in real, live conversations and live events can be an excellent method of promoting our message and selling more books.

For some, this approach will be a natural fit, but for others, speaking before a crowd or interacting with readers one-on-one will seem impossible. Although hiding behind a social media platform may feel "safer," you can have success in face-to-face marketing opportunities. The fact we call this phenomenon "social media" is interesting because these platforms do not offer the opportunity for a real, meaningful relationship. Live events, however, offer a platform for new relationships, which may also mean more sales.

You probably know I have the privilege of serving as pastor to a congregation in Georgia. I don't see live events as just marketing moments. They are also ministry moments, much like what I experience through preaching on any given Sunday. When I interact with individuals or crowds of people, I have the opportunity to pour into their lives and encourage life change. You have the same opportunity. We all have messages about which we are passionate. At live events, your chance to invoke growth and change in the lives of readers is much greater than just through lit screens of computers across our globe.

As an author, you can pursue a variety of different face-to-face encounters. I realize these opportunities can be time consuming and difficult to fit into our schedules. You'll have to be selective so you're using your time wisely, but the impact of live events can be profound. You will interact with readers and see how live events can impact book sales. In this chapter, we'll focus on steps we should take in preparing for event marketing. In the next chapter, we'll look at utilizing the platform of public speaking and additional ways to have face-to-face encounters with readers.

Before You Go into the Public

You can't start speaking to crowds or get behind an author's table and sign books without preparing. Preparation is important. Remember the old axiom *You never get a second chance to make a good first impression.* If you have opportunity to speak to a crowd of people about the topic of your book, make sure you're ready to make a good first impression.

Of course, it's not just about impressions. It's about authenticity. Marketing, and life for that matter, is about other people, not us. In our preparation, we have to get ready to offer something of value to others that will be significant and helpful.

I once heard a story about preaching that I've applied to relationships. A man went to hear two great preachers in London. He left the first thinking, "What a great preacher." He left the second thinking, "What a great God." As a preacher, this story makes me ask the question of myself, "Do I reveal the greatness of God in my preaching?" This story not only makes me think about preaching but also makes me question my interactions with people in general. What do they think when they walk away from me? Am I the main topic of our conversation or is the person I'm talking to the main topic? Hopefully, they will feel loved, valued, and resourced.

How will you prepare? First, know your subject. If you are speaking on a platform or connecting one-on-one with people at an author's signing table, be ready to communicate about the topic of your book. Granted, one-on-one conversations can go in many directions that have nothing to do with your book, but make sure you're prepared to have those key conversations that connect readers back to the message of your book.

> *"By failing to prepare, you are preparing to fail."*
> Benjamin Franklin

If you're like me, by the time your book comes out in paperback, you may be writing your next book. It may take me eight months to a year (or longer) to write a book and publish it. I'll preach forty-five or more times during that year plus speak to various groups. Because I wrote a book on a topic doesn't mean I always have that message in the forefront of my mind. I suggest creating a short summary of your book that includes the high points. If someone asks specific questions about your book, you'll be prepared to talk with them and not later regret having forgotten things you should have said.

Remember *it's not about you*. Most people's favorite topic is themselves. You will go further in life and in accomplishing your goals as a writer if you make sure you focus on the person, or persons, to whom you speak. If it's a personal conversation, ask questions about the other person that will help them process the principles of your book without sounding like you're focusing on your book or your expertise. Be prepared to help them see how your book will help them. People will not buy your book to assist you in becoming a bestseller. They will buy your book to meet a need in their lives.

People don't care so much what your book is about as much as what your book will do for them. If they ask you about your book and you answer with a long response regarding plot or a list of key principles and concepts of your book, you'll lose them and lose a reader. I mentioned in chapter six you should prepare a one-sentence response when people ask about your book, but your response should show them how they'll benefit from your book.

I told you when they ask what my novels are about, I say, "I write books that help people imagine and experience the kinds of relationships they've always wanted to have." I'll say that first when someone wants to know about my book. Then, I'll say in another sentence my stories reveal those relationships through suspense and adventure that include scuba diving, treasure hunting, and intrigue. I may tap into the theme of a particular book as well. For example, *Finding My Way* and *Ready to Love Again* tells the story of a young girl struggling to have a meaningful relationship because of abuse and relationship failures in her past.

Also, before going into public, have some book markers or small book promotion cards ready. I have business card size promotions that have a picture of one of my book covers on one side and the picture of another book cover on the other side. On the bottom of the card is a reminder to readers they can find this book on Amazon or any other retailer, and I offer a shortened link connected to my Amazon Associate account (I'll cover this concept in Chapter Nineteen). You may want to have a picture of the cover on one side and a book description on the other. Book markers give you enough space to highlight more than one book. I use Got Print (gotprint.com) to print most of my promotional pieces.

Be careful to make sure you're not always saying, "Buy my book" through your conversations or speaking engagements, but make sure people know you have a book. Printed material can be that subtle invitation to purchase your book. It's possible they can't buy your book then, but the book marker will be a reminder.

Also, create an author business card. Your business card should include your author picture, a brief statement that summarizes your purpose and genre, your name, website, and contact information. On the back, I include pictures of a few of my book covers. Here is a picture of the front of one of my author business cards:

Preparing a Media Kit

Imagine you're an event coordinator for a group of authors and you come across my book on marketing. You begin to think about asking me to speak to your group about writing and publishing, but you need to do more homework to make sure I'm the right guy. You could read over my bio on Amazon or study the homepage of my website, but that may not be enough. You need something that gives you detail about me and offers a resource to promote your event. A media kit, or demo kit, is a resource that combines a lot of information about the author so a person can go to one place to find out information about the author and his or her book. It's like a business card on steroids.

This collection of information is also a media resource a magazine editor could review to write up a short article about you or your book. Book reviewers and bookstore personnel may use it to gain additional information to write a review about you and your book or to prepare for a book sign-ing event. If you're speaking at an event, someone can use the information in your kit to prepare to introduce you or to decide which breakout session you might be best suited to lead.

The term *media kit* sounds like a collection of material put together in a physical package. It could be that, but in the digital age, it may not be a physical package. You may create a collection of digital material and place it under a tab on your website or as a download for those who are interested. So, what goes into a media kit?

- Author Photo - Include a high resolution, professional picture that offers the quality needed for a poster or video presentation. Notice I said "professional." Most people have quality cameras these days, so I realize we can get quality pictures on our own. Make sure you don't skimp on this piece. Don't use a group picture and crop everyone else out of it. It should be good quality. This picture should be the one you use for all your publications. Remember you are your brand, and your familiar face is part of that brand. Use the same picture for all of your marketing.

- Author Bio - Create a one-page that introduces you to readers and to people who may be in charge of securing a speaker for an event. Give your background that makes you qualified to write what you write. Tell about your education, your experiences, and your writing. Avoid advertising only yourself. Work to show what you can do for others.

- Speech Topics - Assuming you're going to have public speaking opportunities, share some topics you are qualified or prepared to discuss. These topics can directly or indirectly connect to your book.

- Audio/Video Samples - Include audio or video samples of interviews you've done in the past but only if they are good quality. You don't have to include the entire interview but give enough so others see how you handle yourself with questions.

- Interview Preparation Materials - Some people who want to interview you will go to your media kit to prepare. You can help interviewers by offering ten to fifteen questions they can ask.
- Links - Include links to articles you've published or websites that may include reviews of your book(s).
- Testimonials - Add five to ten testimonies from people about how your writing and speaking have impacted their lives.

Face-to-face encounters can be effective in spreading your message or promoting your book. These encounters come in response to a lot of work on securing the engagement. In the next chapter, we'll consider specific types of public opportunities that can help market your book.

Action Points
- What is your reaction to a public event for marketing your book? Does this idea fit into your comfort zone?
- Look over your book, or future book, and make a list of five topics you think relate to the subject of your book. Imagine giving a talk on these topics and create a general outline of what you may present.
- Earlier in the chapter, I said, "Be prepared to tell people in one sentence why you write, and your comment should show them how they will benefit from buying and reading your book." Create several one-sentence statements you can use when someone asks, "So, what's

your book about?" Remember to make your statements about your reader and not yourself.

- Create an author business card and/or bookmark you can use to promote yourself or your book. Visit gotprint. com to consider having these printed.

- Review the list of items that can go into a media kit. What will you include in yours? Create an author bio so you will have a beginning point for this resource.

- Have a professional headshot taken. If you opt to get someone to use a good quality camera/phone to take this picture, make it as professional as possible.

- Review the information by Westwind Communications on taking a headshot: westwindcos.com/authors-need-great-headshot-tips-get-one.[1]

Chapter Sixteen

Face-to-Face Marketing

Face-to-face marketing can be exhausting and rewarding. You may find it interesting to meet people who have been impacted by your writing, and readers trust someone they've seen or met. This marketing method can end in significant book sales. Speaking to groups will expand your platform, give you the opportunity to build your email database, and possibly provide a helpful honorarium. If your engagement goes well and builds interest in your book, people will not only purchase your book but also tell other people about their experiences at the event. These encounters can lead to more book sales.

Engaging through Speaking Opportunities

Speaking engagements may be the most effective way to connect to large groups of readers. Many organizations are looking for guest speakers every day, and you may be able to meet the needs of a variety of groups. You will find a number of groups within your own community who will be happy to invite you to speak at an event. It may be as simple as asking for the opportunity. If you want to be a successful public speaker, here are principles that will help you.

Connect to the person in charge to get the engagement. If you want to be effective in getting on the calendar, deal with the person in charge. It doesn't help to convince assistants you are the best speaker for a certain event. They are gatekeepers and boss protectors. Speak to the event coordinator, the guest speaker decision maker. You will be able to find out all the information needed as well as convince the coordinator you are the speaker he or she needs. Coordinating with the person in charge will also help you avoid having to make additional phone calls for clarification.

Once you get on someone's calendar as the guest speaker, it's best to follow up with something in writing. If it's the kind of event that requires a contract, send that out within a week of the phone call. It's also best to contact the coordinator again a week or two before the event to verify the time and any details that may have been overlooked.

Be clear and on point. If you want to hit a home run, you better make sure you're playing on the right field. Your message must be one the group needs to hear. The object is not just to speak somewhere but to speak where you can connect and meet needs. It's also important to remember your real purpose is not to sell books. Granted, we all want to sell books, but our purpose is to promote life change in the lives of our listeners. It's best to reference your book in your speech or message but not be obnoxious about it. You may want to offer a gift and invite people to stop by your book table to pick it up. Your "gift" could be a list or resource

> *"It takes far more work to be clear than it does to be confusing."*
> Carey Nieuwhof

also included in your book. You can mention that it's in your book, but you also have a free version you'd like to share. Not only are you being generous, but also you're revealing the kind of content readers will find in your book.

Be concise and on time. There's nothing worse than having a crowd finish before you. We've all been on the receiving end of speeches or sermons that just wouldn't end. No one wins. For those of us who are preachers, we should be careful about blaming God for our long-windedness. Most of the time when we are long-winded, it's not because of God's Spirit but because of our poor preparation (I feel like I just stepped on my own toes). It's important to ask the person in charge how long you can speak and stay under your allotted time. If you don't, you may lose future opportunities. You should think of the one thing you want your listeners to do and make that the focus of your message.

Be relevant and practical. I have to admit I get excited about things that does not interest a lot of people. For pastors, we have to realize there are some things about the Bible that light our fires, but to much of the population, they may be buckets of water on glowing embers. Other speakers can fall into a similar trap regardless of their fields. Just because you're excited about a topic doesn't mean everyone is. We must find ways to convey our messages in a way that connect with listeners. There's a time to share something people need to hear, whether they know it or not, but we also need to make sure our message is addressing real needs our listeners know exist. Our speeches, and books for that matter, should give information and offer practical applications.

Always evaluate. I have a problem of doing something and immediately moving to the next item on my list. I have found as a preacher who preaches almost every week, Sunday comes around with amazing regularity. We have to make ourselves stop and evaluate our last message or pro-

ject. What went well? What didn't go well? Do you feel like
you accomplished your objective? Did people leave with a
specific application in mind? Did you stay within your time
limit? What steps do you need to take in follow-up? Self-
evaluations are difficult because the speaker's perspective is
somewhat limited. It's possible to video yourself and go back
later and evaluate your speech.

As part of this process, you can send a note to the coordinator to thank him or her for the opportunity. Also, ask
for an endorsement you can add to your website.

It's also a good idea to have someone else evaluate you.
This may be difficult to do if you're speaking somewhere and
don't know anyone. My staff and I evaluate our Sunday
morning services every Monday. We try to be blatantly honest about everything. Keep your evaluations in writing so
you can refer to them and work on specific changes for your
next event.

Connecting through Book Signings

Some authors don't like book signings because they take
a lot of time and sometimes do not bring much of a return.
I fall into both of these categories. At the same time, however, it takes only one person to get excited and start something viral about your book on his or her social media platform or to extend a speaking invitation.

You get the opportunity to offer a book signing by asking for it. Many stores are open to allowing you a small space.
They may have various rules. For example, I have found
some stores want to order my books through their channels.
It's easier if you can take a supply of your books, let the store
sell them, and then have the store give you a percentage of

the sales. I find when I do book signings and the store sells the book for me up front, I receive only two to three dollars per book in royalties.

I suggest you take a supply of your books (though don't set out stacks and stacks of them on the table unless you're attending a large event), a bowl of individually wrapped candy pieces, a couple of signing pens (in case one of them quits working), table decorations, tablecloth, price sheet, and breath mints. If the proprietor wants you to finalize the sale of the book instead of having the sale go through the store's normal checkout procedure, you'll need to take change and a credit card reader (I use square at squareup.com). You should ask the proprietor if you need to furnish your own table and chair. I prefer to stand, but that can make for a long and tiring experience.

> *"Personal appearances are a proving ground for your authority and carry immediate rewards."*

Taking Your Message to the Classroom

Teachers often invite guest speakers into the classroom, and you could be one of those guest speakers. I just spoke with a history teacher who will be taking his class through a series of lectures on Mexican history. My fifth and sixth novels of the Davenport Series (by Judah Knight) take place in Mexico and tie to the ancient Meso-American people in Mexico. He invited me to come in as a guest speaker on Mexican history.

Some English teachers may invite you to talk with their students about the writing journey. Be prepared to connect your comments to traditional writing structures and address normal questions about writing challenges (i.e. The hero's journey, active versus passive verbs, writers' block, etc.).

Sometimes, it takes a while to get approval to speak in a school setting. You may have to go through a process with background checks, but the opportunity to influence young people greatly outweighs any related challenges. Book sales with students vary, but you never know whom you may influence and how they may go on to change the world.

Influencing Others through Conferences

Speaking to people gathered for conferences can be exciting for book sales and for expanding your platform and influence. If you are a nonfiction writer, chances are that you'll have greater opportunity for this outlet than fiction writers. Fiction writers, however, may have opportunity to speak at writers' conferences or other conferences that connect to their topic of expertise.

To be a guest speaker at a conference, you'll have to be recognized as an expert in your field or, at least, as someone who has something of value to offer to conferees. Create a page in the back of your book suggesting the reader invite you to speak at their next event. Offer the means by which they can contact you and create a link to your media page, which offers suggestions on topics you can cover.

You can market yourself to conference organizers. I suggest connecting with leaders of conferences you attend. Let them know you are available to speak and share with them through printed material, or your website, why you'll be a good fit. Connect with the leadership while at the conference and send a follow-up email offering your services. In your brief email, point them to your website that introduces you as a qualified speaker.

Money, Money, Money

One of the great challenges of beginning conference speakers is money. What will you charge? In the early stages, you may need to offer your services for free. Eventually, you'll need to set a price for your services. Your fee should include travel expenses plus honorarium. It's important to take into account the time you need to prepare for the engagement as well as the travel time and engagement commitment. Once at the point when you can expect pay for your speaking engagements, you could leave the amount up to the coordinator, but don't expect it to be an optimum amount. At first, this approach may get your name out into the public and help you sell additional books. As you get more engagements under your belt, you'll be able to raise your fees.

I struggle with having a set fee for my speaking engagements. I leave fees up to the conference organizer or the person in charge. If I was dependent upon making a full-time living as an author, I might take a different approach. People have to function in a way that's best for their objectives.

Regardless of how you choose to handle this issue, be clear. Make sure that your fees or policies are clear from the start so there are no surprises. In your follow-up letter, remind the person in charge of the policy you discussed. If your engagement includes a contract, the amount and financial expectations should be included.

When setting up a speaking engagement, ask if it's appropriate to offer a book table. I prefer not to promote my own products; instead, I ask the people in charge if he or she would like to mention it. I may invite people to the book table after the event for a gift or to sign up for my newsletter (email list), but I am careful not to push book sales. I may reference something in one of my books, but I stay away from anything that sounds like I'm pushing book sales.

Author and marketing coach Rob Eagar mentioned a useful strategy that helps market your books at speaking events. Include a "book marketing tool" in your manuscript. He says, "These tools are nuggets of content designed to spike reader interest that you place in your manuscript deliberately."[1] He suggests this tool offer immediate value to the reader by sharing something new, solving a problem, or offering something humorous. It can include resources, such as reader quizzes, how-to articles, study guides, behind the scenes information, or some other helpful resource. Eagar also suggests we include more than one book marketing tool in the book. I mention this idea because it may be a good marketing tactic to offer one of these resources as a gift at our book table. Tell your audience your book has several useful resources, and you want to share one of these resources with them as a gift. It will show them the kind of materials you offer in the book and becomes a great promotional piece that can lead to more sales.

> "Let's all stop shouting ['Buy My Book'] in a crowd and start having the kind of smaller conversations that actually help us connect as human beings."
> Delilah Dawson

Getting a strong start from the beginning is a key element to successful book sales. Strong sales lead to speaking opportunities, bestseller status, and a greater level of influence. So, how do you start well? We'll look at the importance and strategy of a successful book launch in the next chapter.

Action Points

- A public speaker must be relevant, or he won't be used. Look over your book topic and make a list of five relevant ideas your book addresses.
- If you want to be a public speaker, create a speaker evaluation tool you can use to evaluate yourself after your event. Consider the one I offer on the following page as an example. How can you tweak this resource to fit your needs?
- Make a list of ten places in your area where you can have a book signing. What steps would you need to follow to line up a book signing event at these places? How will you promote it?
- How can your topic be addressed in the classroom? Write out several ways you can connect to students through your writing.
- Review your book or book idea. What book marketing tools can you create to include in your book? If you are a published author, can you add at least three book marketing tools to your book? If you haven't published your book yet, figure out how you can utilize this helpful idea with three book marketing tools before your book goes to print.
- Which book marketing tools did I use within this book?

Public Speaking Evaluation Tool

Face-to-face marketing can be both exhausting and rewarding. You may find it interesting to meet people who have been impacted by your speaking and seek help with your evaluation, but most of the time, you'll have to rely upon your perceptions for an evaluation. You'll find an evaluation tool or process below that may be of help as you work to improve yourself.

You need to consider a variety of questions. What went well? What didn't go well? Do you feel like you accomplished your objective? Did people leave with a specific application in mind? Did you stay within your time limit? What steps do you need to take in follow-up? Rate yourself on the statements below using a scale of 1 – 5 with 5 being the best score.

Preparation

1. My correspondence with the person in charge was adequate.
2. My speech/message was adequately prepared with plenty of time to review my thoughts and notes before the presentation.
3. My notes, if any, were adequate and ready for the presentation.
4. My expectation of the meeting space was accurate.
5. I was well rested (good night's sleep).
6. I was properly attired for the occasion.

7. I planned my travel to arrive early.

8. I arranged for needed presentation equipment in advance.

9. Any visuals I used were well prepared for the event.

10. My choice of topic fit my audience well.

11. I got permission to record my speech to place the recording on my website.

12. I arrived early and performed a sound check with the sound technician.

Delivery

Overall Delivery:

1. I connected to the needs of my audience.

2. I felt comfortable and at ease with the whole experience.

3. I stayed within the scheduled time limits.

4. My audience was engaged with me throughout my speech.

5. I used appropriate and relevant illustrations and quotes during my speech.

6. My speaking tempo was appropriate.

7. I used variety in my delivery - variety of volume, expression, tempo.

8. My body language supported my message.

9. The sections of my presentation were well timed and balanced.

Introduction:

1. I used an effective opening statement that resulted in engagement from my audience.

2. My introduction was an appropriate length for my overall presentation.

3. I set up the listeners' expectation for my presentation with my comments.
4. I concluded my introduction with a good transition into the body of my message.

Main Body:
1. I effectively covered the main topic of my message.
2. My illustrations and quotes were well placed to support my message.
3. My illustrations were balanced, without giving undue attention to myself, and moved my message to its proper conclusion.
4. I paced myself well throughout my message.
5. I used good intonation and varied voice pitch to convey my message with passion and energy.
6. My content was instructive and encouraging.
7. I used visuals to assist in my presentation.

Conclusion:
1. The wording of my conclusion was intentional and focused on the objective of offering a call to action.
2. My timing was well placed and balanced.
3. I summarized my message well and offered a memorable closing quote or illustration.
4. I offered a call to action to my message.

Book "Marketing" through the presentation:
1. I quoted my book(s) at least once during my presentation.
2. I did not push the sale of my books but someone else mentioned my book table.

3. I mentioned the marketing tool in my book and offered a gift to the audience that could be picked up at my book table.
4. I invited my listeners to sign up for my newsletter.

Book Table
1. I had my table set up early enough before the event so as to be able to interact with people before the event started.
2. My table was decorated intentionally and effectively.
3. I had bookmarks and other printed material to share with interested people.
4. I had candy to offer people who stopped by the table.
5. I had a gift to offer people who would sign up for my newsletter.
6. I had enough change to offer people purchasing my book, and I had a means for taking credit/debit cards.
7. I had someone else run my table so I could speak with people freely.

Follow-through
1. I wrote a note of thanks to the person in charge of my event.
2. I asked the event coordinator for a letter of recommendation to include on my website.
3. I wrote a note of thanks and offered a gift to the person running my book table.
4. I included the event coordinator on my list for Christmas greeting cards.

Chapter Seventeen

Book Launch - Part One

At some point in our lives, we've all agreed with the old adage "all's well that ends well." Most of the time, however, what starts well has a better chance of ending well. Even as I type these words, I realize I've already established that marketing should start before we write our book, but our book launches will, at least, feel like the starting line for many of us. When I first began writing and publishing, I saw the launch as something to think about once I completed my manuscript, made final edits, and uploaded my final interior document and cover design for printing. I now realize a book launch needs to start before you type your last period.

You can divide your book launch into several categories: prepublication, publication, post-publication, and a category I'm going to call "revival." Let's look at the first of these four areas, which is the most critical to your launch success. At the conclusion of Chapter Eighteen, I've included a "Book Launch Check List" I think you'll find useful.

Prepublication

I mentioned that the best time to start marketing your book is before you write it. I'll follow that statement up by saying the best time to launch a book is before you publish it. I suppose technically your book can't be launched if it doesn't exist, but your book concept can begin to live long before your printer puts ink to page. You can accomplish this prepublication launch through several means.

Anticipation

Anticipation is a wonderful marketing tool. If you want your book to sell like wildfire, you can't throw a match onto wet wood. A wise marketing strategy will always include plans to alert your reading audience to your upcoming publication and unique nuances of your book. One great advantage of building anticipation is advance interest in your book equals book sales within the first few days of your release date. A surge in sales brings instant recognition by retailers and an enhanced algorithm on Amazon, which means even more sales.

One way to build anticipation is involve readers in some of the details of your writing and publication. You can offer cover options and have people vote on their favorite. You can ask for input on some of the topics in your book and let your audience know some of their comments may show up in your publication. You can offer sneak peeks at pieces of your book. The key is to make sure you have a mechanism in place to give readers updates. I suggest not only getting email addresses whenever possible but also using every social media platform at your disposal. People are bombarded with new information, so if you don't plan to announce your release in such a way that those anticipating your book will know it's available, you may not be as likely to turn anticipation into book sales.

> "Anticipation is the missing ingredient in marketing."
> Jason Martuscello

Interviews offer another means by which you can let people know your book is coming. Some radio stations may invite you to talk about your topic, or you may have public speaking opportunities in advance of your book. You can use these platforms not only to promote your upcoming release but also to offer preorders (which I'll discuss in more detail) to interested readers. One way you can capture email addresses so you will be able to alert people by email of your book release is to offer people your book marketing tool I mentioned in the previous chapter. You can set it up as a pdf download and invite people to go to a certain website to get their free copy. When they go to that website, they'll find the landing page for the free item that offers the gift as a lead magnet that captures their email address.

Launch Team or Street Team

I have no idea who originated the term "street team," but it describes a group of people who are willing to help you market your book. I suppose it's called "street team" because they "hit the streets" to tell everyone about your new release. I'll use the words *street team* and *launch team* interchangeably. I've told groups that just because you self-publish doesn't mean you publish by yourself. The same is true for marketing. Even if you publish through traditional means, you still need a street team to help you be a success.

Your launch team will consist of people who believe in you and your message. It will be people who are willing to spend time and influence in order to help you get the word out about your book.

We just had a Fall Festival at my church that served about 1200 people from our community, and it took about 200 volunteers to pull off the event. We had a booming success on Halloween night, and none of the volunteers were paid a penny. The atmosphere at the event from both attenders and volunteers was joyful. After the inflatables were deflated and attenders left our property, around seventy-five volunteers (maybe more) stayed to help clean up our building, many of whom had been at the church for much of the day setting up. With a little work, we can get similar help with our book launches.

Start with an explanation of the message of your book, presenting the "Why?" before you offer the "What?" to volunteers who may be interested in helping you. Next, create a good job description for street team members so they will know exactly what they're agreeing to do on your behalf. Within your job description, offer a timeline so they'll have a general idea about how long they're serving. I also suggest you present more than one level of participation for street team members.

You will also need a means of communicating with your team members. Email is a great tool, but you can also use Facebook. You can set up a closed group on Facebook and invite people to join your street team group.

> "People don't buy WHAT you do; they buy WHY you do it."
> Simon Sinek

Remember to be consistent and regular in offering updates on your Facebook page and always respond quickly to participants' comments or questions.

One thing you will be asking your street team to do is to post information on social media about your book release. Create visual resources they can use for this task. Develop a reser-voir of memes related to your book and prepare short quotes from your book they can share. Create a timeline they'll need to follow and update your team as to any changes you'll have to make to your plans.

> *"By appreciation, we make excellence in others our own property."*
> *Voltaire*

Send your team members a free advanced copy of your book and ask them to read it and write a review. The review can't be posted until you publish your book, but they can be ready to share the review during the first week of the book's life on Amazon or other retail stores. Don't forget to ask them to post their review on Goodreads. You may want to send them this advanced copy as a pdf download and then send them a copy of your book as a gift and include a personal thank you note written in the front of the book.

You can also offer inexpensive gifts to your team. These gifts could be something such as a coffee mug with a picture of your book cover on it or even a tee-shirt advertising your book. If you spend $10 per team member, you see how quickly this can add up. Fifty team members would cost you $500 plus shipping. Think for a moment, however, about the marketing mileage you'll get out of fifty people who are working hard to promote your book. The investment is well worth it! Let's assume you'll make $5.00 per book in royalties (this is possible with a paperback book). Do you think fifty people will sell 100 books for you? Beyond a doubt!

The key is to enlist your team, stay in touch with them throughout the process, equip them for the job you've asked them to do, and then reward them as a way to say, "thank you." You'll need to do some work on the front end, but your labor will pay dividends in the long run.

Reviews

I've written about gathering reviews, but I suggest you try to gather as many as possible in advance of your release date. Send out advance copies of your book and have people, including your street team, ready to share their review during the first week after the release date. Some people may opt to purchase your book as well so their review will be "verified;" therefore, you should consider offering your digital book for ninety-nine cents on a particular day and let your reviewers know of the special one-day price.

You may also want to purchase reviews from professional reviewers such as Kirkus and Readers' Favorite. You can have these reviews done in advance and include some of the comments in your book or in your promotional material. Amazon will not allow them to be posted under the review section on the sales page, but you can add it to your book description.

Reviews are SO important. I strongly urge you to develop a review strategy and follow it closely.

Preorders

Amazon offers a preorder process for your new releases. It may be challenging, but many authors find it a helpful tool. The problem is that once you lock in your book for preorder (four days before the release date), you can't make any changes to it until after the release date. That means if you find a glaring error in the book after the preordering begins, you can't correct it until after it's live on Amazon. All of the people who purchase the book under prerelease will have a copy with the error in it.

> "In a successful launch, the author believes that buying his or her book is actually a good thing for people to do."
>
> Tim Grahl

Preorders on a digital version of your book can be helpful in that they boost your overall sales numbers. This will improve your metrics on Amazon and help you to gain exposure. In full disclosure, I've only offered a book for preorder once. I discovered a major mistake after the preorder deadline, and a number of people purchased a flawed version of the book. I plan to try it again on this book with more intentional marketing behind the effort and greater attention to my final edit before locking the book down in preorder.

You can offer a preorder with paperback copies, but at this point, it will require you mailing the paperback books out after the release date instead of relying on Amazon or another retailer doing it for you. IngramSpark, however, is one service that offers preorder sales in paperback. One advantage to offering a preorder in paperback *you* send out after you release your book is that you can send an autographed copy to those interested.

Using preorders as a part of your marketing strategy has several advantages. One is that you can start marketing your book earlier and build anticipation of its release date. You will also have a growth in sells building up to your release date. This boost in sales could help you to become a best-seller, and your Amazon algorithms will reflect this surge.

One strategy in making sales ahead of publishing is you need to create scarcity with your new book. The problem is your book will be available after the preorder period, so a lot of people may wait to make the purchase. You can solve this dilemma by offering a special gift or bonus material for those who preorder. Once people preorder your book, they can email a receipt to an address created for the occasion, and the bonus gift can be sent out to them. Once the release date arrives, the bonus material is no longer available. In addition to a preorder sale, you'll also gain a reader's email address.

Action Points

- How can you build anticipation for your book? Make a list of five things you can do to involve readers in your book content long before it's ever published.
- Have you created your gift, your lead magnet, that you offer readers in order to get their email addresses for future email marketing? Think of a resource you can tie to your book's theme and make sure it's ready before publication. You'll need to include links to your landing page in the front and rear of your book in a prominent location (see Chapter Thirteen).

- Make a list of at least twenty-five people you can ask to be on your street team.
- Create a job description for your street team members and a letter you can include in an email to enlist them to help you with your launch. I've offered a sample after Chapter Eighteen.
- What gift can you offer your street team members? It can't be too expensive, but you also want it to represent your gratitude.
- In addition to your street team, can you think of twenty people you can ask to read your book and be prepared to post a review as soon as the book comes out? Make a list and be prepared to contact them more than once.
- What special gift or bonus material can you offer to people who preorder your book? Create a deadline on your calendar when you plan to have this material ready.

Chapter Eighteen

Book Launch - Part Two

We've all heard the journey of a thousand miles begins with one step. Let's say the first step of the marketing journey, as it pertains to the launch, is the prelaunch activities I shared in the last chapter. You may feel overwhelmed after reading that chapter, and that first step may have been exhausting. Don't give up. Keep your eyes on the prize.

What is the prize? You should figure that out and write down your launch goals. The prize could be 100 reviews, one thousand books sold in the first four weeks, landing multiple speaking engagements whereby you influence others with your message, or bringing in a certain amount of money through your first month's royalties.

How can you stay strong during your book's release? Keep your eyes on the prize! Look at your goals often, develop a step-by-step strategy to accomplish your goals, and celebrate each win. Although your prepublication phase is critical, the next phases are also important.

Publication

The start of this phase is defined by the actual publishing of your book. This phase of the launch strategy should last a month or so. Day one of your new book's life is a critical day. You need sales, reviews, and publicity. If you offered preorders of your book, you may gain momentum that will give you a bump in sales at your launch. You can also offer an additional gift through your marketing for the first week, as I mentioned under the section on preorders.

Your street team will be critical during the publication phase. Contact the members several days before the launch with a countdown to launch day. You can have focused promotional pieces in your prelaunch material for the last few days but also provide promotional material for launch day. Stay in touch with your team, thanking them for their work and help. Continue to offer marketing resources each day for the first week or so. Also, send out a thank you gift to your street team during the first couple of weeks. You can find a number of personalized gifts on a site like 4imprint. com or positivepromotions.com.

The first thirty days are important to a book's life and opportunity for long-term success. If you can manage to hit the bestseller list in your category and stay on that list for at least several days (the longer the better), your Amazon algorithm will be greatly affected, and you'll discover Amazon advertising your book for you at no cost. If you have great success during the first month of your launch, you may have a successful second month.

> *"You cannot expect people to buy your products or services if you won't invest in yourself."*
> Brendon Burchard

Your first thirty days are an important time to be spreading the word about your book through interviews, guest blogs, and podcasts. To tap into the resource of other people's blogs and podcasts, you'll have to connect with bloggers and interviewers well in advance of your release.

The more focused your audience is to your topic, the better your success. For example, it will not help me to be interviewed for this book on a podcast that targets readers of romance. For this book, I need to target authors.

Set a goal for how many reviews you want to receive during the first week. Get as many reviews as possible the first days. Good reviews sell books! Will you consider stopping now and writing a review for this book on Amazon and Goodreads? Thanks in advance for your review.

One of the items on your street team's job description is to post reviews of your book on Amazon, Goodreads, and other possible services. Follow up with them and thank them for the review. You can also email people who preordered your book. You'll get their email addresses by offering them a bonus gift if they email you their receipt. Thank them for purchasing your book. Ask them if they enjoyed your book and would be willing to write a review. Send out a newsletter to your email list at least once a week during the first thirty days. Offer free information and gifts to your readers. Don't always ask for something, but you can periodically request a review.

You also want to send out press releases to be published during your first week. These releases can go to newspapers, bloggers, and anyone else who may be interested in letting the world know about your book. I've had success in having articles written in my local newspaper about my book releases. I usually write the article and submit it in advance.

Finally, schedule several book launch events. Start with a launch party and invite everyone who helped you write, publish, and promote your book. Invite anyone who is interested in celebrating the release of your book. Maybe you can time your launch party when you can join another author who's celebrating his release as well. I've had some success with doing a launch event with other authors and found new readers who otherwise would not have known about my book. You can also do a virtual event by inviting people to join you online. I have used Facebook for this purpose and interacted with people in real time, discussing my newest book. Your followers may help you significantly.

Post-publication

This phase begins about two months after publication and lasts for at least a year or two. We hope our books continue to live and thrive for many years, but it depends upon our marketing work during post-publication. I have found with consistent work, our books can enjoy a long shelf life with growing success.

Your street team will have to be released at some point. You can't lean on them for too long during this phase. Stay in touch with them, though. Give them updates and correspond with them about future projects. Remember that getting their help requires you establish a win-win relationship. They need to know you experienced success because of their significant efforts.

Continue to work on getting reviews. ALWAYS work at getting reviews. It's easy to grow slack by thinking readers will automatically write reviews. It doesn't happen often. I may sell hundreds of books before one person leaves a review, so getting reviews takes a lot of effort..

Do your best to line up speaking events related to your book. An event can be a book signing at the local coffee shop or speaking to a business club during its monthly lunch meeting. Look for conferences in your state where your topic fits the theme and objectives of the gathering. You'll need to work on this objective long before your publication, but conference speaking will expand your influence and sell more books.

Writing is fun. Rewriting is challenging. Marketing is difficult. However, book sales come to those who work hard at marketing. Develop a schedule for posting on social media and marketing through paid email services. Don't let up, and you'll reap the benefits.

Revival

To revive something means to bring new life. At some point, your book will be old news, but that doesn't mean you have a funeral service for it. Some readers are looking for a new book, so your old copyright date may discourage sales. A decline in sales is natural, but it's possible to bring new life to old books.

If you think about it, one reason your book did so well during the publication and post-publication phases was because you worked hard. As you become consumed with writing your next book, it's easy to slack up on marketing your previous book, and your previous book slips into no man's land. One strategy to move your old book into a season of revival is to go back to the steps you took during the early days of your book's life and do them again. They worked before, and they will work again.

Pastor Charles M. Sheldon wrote *In His Steps* in 1896 and sold over 100,000 copies in the first few weeks after publication. It became the bestselling novel of the nineteenth century. By 1935, it had been translated into twenty-one languages, and by 1956 over eight million copies were sold. Due to a copyright mistake, the book was published freely around the world, and some have estimated over thirty million copies sold worldwide. In 1964 Ken Anderson films released a movie based on the novel. Sheldon's grandson created an updated version of the story, and in the 1990s, a youth pastor created the WWJD (What Would Jesus Do) bracelets that sold like wildfire. In 2010, another movie was released, and it is now estimated that over 50,000,000 copies of the book have been sold. Can old books find new life? You'd better believe it!

> "Talent is not enough to guarantee success. If you want longevity and prosperity as an author, it all comes down to one word: Platform!"
> Collins, Hall & Rhodes

Although you may not sell millions of copies, a revival of your old book is possible. The real question is how? First, I must say it will more likely happen by following an intentional strategy. You can get your book back in front of new readers. I'll mention a few steps you can take to create a revival of your book.

- **Create a marketing blitz tied to a new book.** It's possible you can write a second book connected to the theme of the first and stir new interest in your older book. This tactic is easy with fiction. A lot of people enjoy reading books in a series when they already know and love the characters. You can follow this same principle in nonfiction as well. Instead of writing one book that's 70,000 words long, consider writing two books at 35,000 words. Your marketing efforts for your second book will breathe new life into your older publication.

- **Create additional resources tied to your older book.** For example, if it is a Christian book, you can turn it into a small group study by creating a small group study guide. You could develop a video teaching series as well. You'll find this strategy easier for nonfiction than fiction, but it's possible to utilize it for both. Because much of the story in the last two books of my *Davenport Series* takes place in Mexico, I've considered creating a travel book on that part of the country as well as a book of authentic Mexican recipes.

- **Republish your older book as a new edition.** Rick Warren took this approach with his book *The Purpose Driven Life*. Warren wrote the book in 2002, republished it with updates, and gave it the title *What On Earth Am I Here For*. As of 2019, the book has sold over thirty-four million copies. How can you update your book with new information to create a second edition? Can you change the title and create a new cover?

- **Publish your older book in a book set with similar books.** If you've written a series, create a box set of the series. If it is a stand-alone book, join forces with other authors who have older books with similar themes.

- **Always include a marketing piece about your older books in your newer publications.** Don't miss the chance of letting new fans know you have additional books. Add pictures of your older books in the final pages of your new book and include monetized links (I'll discuss this in the next chapter) where readers can purchase them.

The harder you work on the front end of your new book's life, the longer it will enjoy record sales. I was slow to learn this lesson in the early stages of publishing and marketing, so I'm passing it along to you. Don't be in too big of a hurry to publish your book. Make sure you have developed a solid launch plan. A good book plus S.M.A.R.T. goals (Specific, Measurable, Achievable, Realistic, and Time-oriented), plus strategies to accomplish the goals, plus a lot of hard work equals many book sales, greater influence, and regular monthly royalty paychecks.

Action Points

- Are you working on a new book? Create meaningful, visual promotion pieces your street team can use to help you promote it. If you don't have a new book coming out in the next year or so, create these promotional pieces for your last book.
- How many reviews do you want for your next book? Create a launch strategy for getting at least twenty reviews for your next book.
- What can you do at your next book launch party? Come up with a list of creative ideas you want to incorporate. How will you make the event fun and memorable?

Whom will you invite? Where will you hold the event? Develop an agenda for the evening.

- How would you like to sell 50 million copies of one of your older books, like Charles Sheldon did? What can you do to revive an older book from your previous publications? If you don't have an older book, make a list of ways you can apply these principles in the future.

- I'm offering a "Book Launch Kit" as a gift to you. Please click this link or visit greentreepublishers.com/book-launch-kit.html to get this helpful resource. It includes a book launch checklist, emails, promotional pieces, and everything I've used to launch this book.

Launch Team

(The following resource is a note and job description I used to enlist my launch team for this book. I offer it as an example.)

Thank you for your willingness to consider being a part of the launch team for my new book, *The Next Bestseller.* This book will be a tremendous help to a lot of authors, and I'm so excited to release it. It was birthed out of my own journey to become a published author and represents some challenges I'm still working to overcome in my own book marketing efforts. Below, you'll find a few keys to what it means to be a part of a launch team.

Why This Book?

Authors typically write books because they have an important message to share. They may be good writers, but many of them do not know how to market their books. Because their marketing skills are lacking, the important message of their books has limited influence. I've written this book to help authors be successful at marketing their books and sharing their messages.

What's a Launch Team?

A launch team is a group of volunteers who believe in the message and mission of an author and are willing to donate some time to help the author launch his or her new book.

If you are willing to be a part of the team, please send me an email letting me know of your willingness. I will communicate with the launch team through emails and text messages. I'll be sending updates and reminders throughout the process.

Responsibilities…

Launch team members can serve at various levels in order to help me spread the word about this new book.

Level 1 –

* Assist me during prelaunch by sharing ideas that will help the book to be a success.
* Get a free copy of the book from me and, if possible, read it before launch day. I can email you the book in pdf format. Be prepared to submit a review to Amazon and Goodreads during the first few days of the launch. If you find any mistakes while you're reading, please submit the mistakes to me so I can correct the book before it's released.
* Consider purchasing a digital copy on a discount day (usually for 99 cents) so your review will be designated "verified" by Amazon. I hate asking for you to purchase the book after you have it, but the "verified" status carries a lot of weight. I'll let you know when I'll offer a discount day.
* You will need to turn through around 25% of the pages of your book before submitting your review. Some retailers know whether or not you've turned through the pages, and they may not think you've read it if you don't take the time to complete this

step. If you don't turn the pages, it's possible your review will not be posted.

- For the review, give the book a star rating (1 – 5), come up with a brief title that summarizes your comments, and share a few sentences that include comments about the book's content. What did it mean to you? What could it mean to another author?

- Help me spread the word through social media that my new book is coming. I will provide special posts you can use, and you can create additional ones.

- Help me get additional reviews. Reviews help sell the book to readers as good or better than any other thing we can do.

Level 2 –

- Assist me in promoting the book through your social media channels during the prelaunch days in order to build anticipation.

- Respond to my posts on social media in order to help create interest. Share your honest thoughts with me through social media so people will get a feel for the content of the book.

- Join me in posting promotional pieces during the first week or two of the launch.

- Continue helping me get additional reviews by asking people on my behalf.

- I will provide you with some promotional memes, videos, and posts you can use during prelaunch (about 2-4 weeks before launch day) and during the first week or so of the launch. The more social media coverage the book can get the better.

Level 3 -

- Continue offering support through the first month or two of the launch by helping me to promote the book and continue to get reviews.
- Help me connect to bloggers and promoters. Any additional media coverage will be helpful.
- Help me evaluate the launch so I can learn how to improve it for my next book launch.

Time Frame...

The time period members of a launch team agree to help an author varies. A "Level 3" volunteer could serve for a total of two to three months, whereas, a "Level 1" volunteer may be finished after posting reviews during the first week of the launch. The prelaunch period lasts about four weeks. The first two weeks after the release are critical and the first four weeks are considered the launch period. Post launch would apply to the months following the initial launch period. I am grateful for any level of help you can offer.

Thanks again for being willing to help the message in my newest book be a success. Many authors have important messages, and this book will equip them with how to spread their messages to potential readers. I'm praying that you will experience a special blessing during this launch period.

Chapter Nineteen

Riding the Internet Wave

Odds are you don't consider yourself to be a famous person. We live in a time when being famous is no longer just a possibility for those who are born into a famous family or who enjoy certain breaks in their lives. The internet has made fame a possibility to anyone who's willing to work at it. I confess that fame is not my objective, but larger influence is.

I stopped at a dive shop in Mexico a couple of years ago to get information about doing some scuba diving on one of the owners' dive boats. I told the dive master I was doing research for my next novel and needed to dive some of the best spots off the coast of Veracruz. He asked my author name, and to my surprise, he knew me from my books. In his mind, I was famous, and he introduced me to everyone in the shop. He became my personal diving guide, and we go to dinner every time I'm in Mexico. Thanks to the internet, my influence has reached places I'd never imagined.

Because you can connect with millions of people around the world by tapping a few keys on your computer, you have the opportunity to sell books anywhere in the world. I remember the shock I experienced when I discovered my book, *Songs from the Heart: Meeting with God in the Psalms*, was selling regularly in the United Kingdom, France, India, and Australia. I wasn't marketing in those countries, but Amazon was doing it for me.

How do you tap into the power of this great resource called the internet? How can you benefit financially through your marketing efforts? I've already written about this issue somewhat in my chapters on social media and building your website, but I'll address additional thoughts about utilizing the power of the internet in this chapter.

Digital Book Promotion Sites

The internet landscape is dotted with promotion sites such as Bookbub or Ereader News Today. These types of sites invite readers to sign up for regular emails promoting digital books (usually books on sale). The better services have readers pick genres they prefer to read and market books to those readers based upon their preferences. Authors can advertise their books to thousands of people and can expect a number of sales. I have found the most accomplished site is Bookbub. It's very difficult to get your book included with Bookbub, but if you do, they are able to predict an approximate number of sales you can anticipate. When I advertise with them, I can expect to sell around 2000 books or more. Remember your book will need to be offered at a discount, so 2000 books sold at ninety-nine cents doesn't mean a huge royalty.

> "If you're going to be the chief marketing officer for your wow product, you must think bigger than you ever have before."
> Michael Hyatt

However, you will experience the results of such a success for a long time after the promotion ends.

When I run promotions, I line up five to seven of the main promotion sites over a course of five or six days. My goal is to hit the bestseller ranking on Amazon on the first day of the promotion and maintain that position until after the promotion ends. If you can manage to accomplish that goal, you'll find Amazon will promote your book for a while, and you'll continue to enjoy success.

I think it's best to run a digital promotion once every two or three months. If your book is enrolled in the KDP Select, you're allowed to offer the discount only once every ninety days. I usually begin my promotion on my own through Facebook ads and pay-per-click marketing on Amazon a few days before the promotion begins. Hopefully, I'll begin building sales before my actual sale starts, and then on the first day of the promotion, I'll sell one hundred or more books, moving my book into the coveted bestseller ranking. You can also time your promotion with an email to your own followers as well as additional Facebook posts.

Here is a list of the best promotion sites that I've found:
- Bookbub - bookbub.com/partners/overview
- Ereader News Today - ereadernewstoday.com
- Bargain Booksy - bargainbooksy.com/for-authors
- Kindle Nation Daily - indie.kindlenationdaily.com
- Book Gorilla - bookgorilla.com/author (You can also get a free post with Book Gorilla when you line up a promotion with Kindle Nation Daily.)
- The Fussy Librarian - thefussylibrarian.com/advertising/making-book-marketing-easier/
- Choosy Bookworm - choosybookworm.com/promote-your-ebooks/

- Ereader Cafe - theereadercafe.com/promote-your-books/

Promotion Services for Christian authors:
- Faithful Reads - faithfulreads.com/authors/
- Gospel ebooks - gospelebooks.net/submit/

You'll find this post on Paid Author to be a helpful discussion of some of the top promotion sites available to you: paidauthor.com/best-ebook-promotion-sites. This page is updated at least every year in order to stay current.

Other People's Platform

According to Pew Research, only ten percent of Americans don't use the internet.[1] This statistic means most people in the United States have some type of platform or online presence. You can put digital promotion sites into this category, but I want you to think about people you know, those connected to your network, or those you will be able to connect to in the future. You may find a number of people will lend their platforms to you to help your book become a better success. Don't be afraid to ask.

Social Media Connections

I'm assuming by now you are utilizing at least one or two social media platforms, so you already have friends or followers. Your friends with whom you connect on social media may be your first line of marketing strength. Review what I shared in the chapter on social media and don't forget we never use these platforms ONLY to promote our books. However, you do have friends, and more than likely, your friends will be willing to help promote your book. If you have 500 Facebook friends who are willing to mention your book in a post, and they each have 500 friends, you could potentially reach 250,000 people with a marketing piece about your book.

Book Blogs

A number of people enjoy blogging about books they've read. I've had several of my books reviewed and shared by bloggers I've never met before, but these reviews helped me connect to their audience. You can find some of these blogs on Facebook or simply by searching for them on Google. I Googled the words "Christian Book Blogs" and discovered quite a list. I'm sure you can find a list of book blogs in your particular genre.

Virtual Book Tours

In the past, authors would board a bus or a plane and travel around the country on a book tour. You still may want to do that, but you can also do a virtual tour online. You can tap into bloggers or podcasters and share a brief message about your book. You may be able to connect to people on Facebook and have them host a "Meet and Greet" with their friends to answer questions about your book.

Online Bookstores and Promotions

You will find a number of resources online that help promote your book. Some may be bookstores, willing to list your book, while others could be promotional sites, such as Bookbub or Readers' Favorite, that allow authors to post their books for readers to see. Posting your book on many sites will give you a larger internet presence, which gives people more hits when they Google your name. Take advantage of every site that offers to list your books. Use their platform to enlarge yours.

Pay-Per-Click Marketing

Pay-per-click marketing means the people or company advertising a product will post an advertisement and pay for every time their ad is clicked. An author can create a visual advertisement on a search engine-based website promoting his book, like Facebook, Amazon, or Google. When a customer clicks on the ad, he'll be taken to the page where he can purchase the book or learn more about the product. The advertiser pays nothing unless the advertisement is clicked.

This type of advertising can be effective, especially when coupled with target-based placement. By target-based, I mean the advertiser can describe to the search engine the type of customer who would like to see his advertisement. For example, on Facebook, you can describe your customer based upon likes and preferences. You can target someone who is in a certain age range, is a certain sex, or enjoys a particular type of entertainment. Your goal is to make sure your ad gets on the screen in front of people most likely to purchase your book.

You can see how profitable this type of targeted advertising can be. Because it's so popular, many people use it. You may be wondering how so many people can get ads on a certain person's computer screen. The answer is you bid for the position. You determine how much you're willing to pay for each click. If you win the bid or auction, your

advertisement is placed in the targeted spots. For example,
you may decide it's worth paying
twenty-five cents to Amazon to
have someone click on the ad that
promotes your book. Amazon
will suggest what a certain keyword is worth, so you're not just
picking an amount out of the air.
Every time that ad is clicked, you
will be billed twenty-five cents.

> "Pay per click is an effective option if you want to reach people who are actively searching for terms related to your [book]."
> DMI Daily Digest

For this type of advertising to
work, you'll need to make sure
once someone goes to your sales page you have convincing
information that leads them to make the purchase. Having
the right kind of sales page means you should have plenty of
good reviews, carefully worded sales copy describing your
book, and an engaging cover graphic.

Monetizing Your Efforts

You can also generate passive income online by tapping
into companies or people who will pay you to advertise their
product. One easy way to earn passive income is through
affiliate marketing. For example, Amazon has a program
whereby you become an Amazon associate. You get a small
commission from a sale on Amazon when someone purchases a product by using a link you provide. I emphasize
the word "small," but pennies add up. Whenever I promote
my books, or other books, I use a link I get from my Amazon
Associate account. Even if someone buys *my* book from
Amazon by following my given link, I get an extra payment.

If I write a blog about a product or mention someone else's book, I use my associate link.

One great benefit is if someone follows your link to Amazon and looks at your book but moves on to purchase a part for their car, you get a cut of that purchase. For twenty-four hours, Amazon remembers you sent this customer to their site, and you get credit for all of their purchases. I met one person who writes blogs on a variety of popular products and makes a good income as an affiliate marketer. I won't be taking a vacation on what I make, but I do get a small amount sent to my bank account every month. Because my name is attached to whatever I promote, I choose not to market something I don't like and affirm.

You can also become an affiliate for other products through a service such as JVZoo. You can promote someone's training course or product and get a nice cut from the sale. I've done this for services I believe in and received as much as fifty percent of the sale. When the cost is around $300, that's a nice paycheck. Some people make a significant amount of money through this method.

The Sky's the Limit

You can find other wonderful ways to tap into the internet to promote your book, and I'm confident we will see new ideas presented to us in the future. You can discover many additional strategies I didn't mention such as webinars, additional paid advertising, and careful keyword placement on websites and advertisements that will draw customers to your book promotions. As we move into the future, we'll find new and effective ways to spread the word about our books and to expand our influence.

Action Points

- Visit several of the book promotion sites, such as Book-bub, Ereader News Today, or Fussy Librarian. Go ahead and set up an author account through Bookbub. Review the process for listing your book.

- How can you tap into other people's platforms? Make a list of people you know or links you may have to other people's audiences. Depending upon your genre, I may be willing to host one of your guest blogs. Contact me on my website at timriordan.com.

- Did you include possible book blogs in the previous point? Google "book blogs" for your genre and make a list of bloggers with whom you'll try to connect.

- Spend a few minutes researching pay-per-click ads on Facebook, Amazon, and Google. Find one on Amazon and click it in order to see how it works.

- Are you interested in becoming an Amazon Associate? Sign up for your account now (affiliate-program. amazon.com/welcome/getstarted).

Chapter Twenty

Putting It All Together

How do you feel after reading the previous pages? Overwhelmed? It's easy to look at the challenge before you and feel like an ant in Walmart on Black Friday. Accomplishing your goal is not hopeless. You can do it.

I considered starting this chapter out by welcoming you to the first chapter. One problem with getting to the last chapter of a book is we tend to think that we're about through. The fact is you are just beginning. Avoid the temptation of completing this book, putting it on your shelf, and moving on to the next book on your list. What will you do with the information you've read and the experiences you've had while reading this book? How will you implement the principles I have shared so you can have success as a published author?

Marketing your book may seem like a drudgery and will make the list of things you hate to do. After a while, you'll connect marketing to the success you're experiencing. You'll get an email from someone whose life was changed because of your book, or you'll get an invitation to speak somewhere as an expert on the topic of your book. You'll begin to realize marketing isn't so bad after all. Right now, you need to figure out what to do next.

With God's Help, I Can

First of all, you may need a pep talk. Somehow, my parents raised me to have an "I can" attitude. I've accepted a little phrase as a constant reminder of a great verse in the Bible, "I can do all things through Christ who strengthens me." My phrase is, "With God's Help, I Can!" You may want to print that phrase out and post it around your house and office. You can become a bestselling published author. It may not happen tomorrow or even the day after, but if you put to practice some of the principles of this book, you'll find success standing on your doorstep.

Your attitude can either be a great benefit or a terrible liability. Start with your attitude. I grew up saying, "If _____ can do it, then so can I." The blank is the name of someone else. I know that philosophy is flawed. For example, if Michael Jordan can dunk a basketball from the free throw line, so can I. I realize we have to be careful whom we put in the blank, but the fact is if someone else can self-publish a book and become a bestselling author, then so can you. If someone else can make a full-time living as a writer, so can you. If someone else can influence people around the world through writing a book, so can you. With God's help, you can!

Once your attitude is in check, you've got to figure out the next steps. I'm offering this final chapter as a resource to help you take the next step and turn your book into a bestselling book.

What's Your Dream?

This question is a great place to start. I've heard only five percent of people write down their goals, but of those who write down their goals, ninety-five percent of them accomplish their goals. Go to Office Depot or Walmart and buy a nice journal. Start on the first page by writing down your goals as an author. Imagine you are being interviewed five years from now by a writer for *Writers' Digest Magazine*, and the interviewer asks you a series of questions:

- Describe for our readers where you were as an author five years ago and what triggered the change in your life that put you on the road to success?
- Aspiring writers look up to you as a huge success. What does success mean to you? How would you define it?
- What is your greatest success as a published author?
- How many books have you written and sold over the last five years?
- What is the secret to your success?
- What disciplines did you develop in your life to become a bestselling author?
- What advice would you offer aspiring writers that might lead to success?

Do the Essentials

Everything in this book is important, but not everything is essential. I'm assuming you understand a prerequisite to success is creating a well-written, relevant book that has the potential to change lives, influence people, entertain folks, or educate readers. Besides a good book, what are the essentials of becoming a successful author? I'd like to mention some things I think are essential, and I want you to consider my list. You can create your own list.

- What's your mission? Write out an author mission statement that will define what you write, who your target audience will be, and what you want to accomplish through your writing. This exercise will help you define your brand and determine who your readers will be (Chapters Five and Six). This process will also challenge you to do your best job to write an excellent book other people want to read.

- Create a solid, excellent website. Because your website is your author storefront and one of the key ways many people will come to know you, don't neglect giving this piece of the marketing puzzle your best shot. If you have to, pay someone to do it for you, but I think with a little work, you can create an effective website yourself. You may also want to take steps to incorporate video on your website (see Chapter Eight and Fourteen).

- Choose one or two social media platforms and master them. You can't be everything to everyone, so just choose one or two. Decide now to become an expert on using a couple of these platforms. Read some books on your platform of choice and begin increasing your proficiency.

- Begin building your email marketing list. Because every successful author I know says I should use email marketing, I think I should sit up and take notice. What gift can you create as a lead magnet to use to get other people's email addresses? Even if your book is not completed yet, go ahead and create this free gift. Sign up with an email marketing service and begin getting new subscribers. Send out a monthly newsletter to your followers and small emails in between monthly mail outs.

- Build your Author Central page on Amazon. You can always tweak it to make it better but start now connecting with readers through this page. As you get ready to publish your book, work hard at making sure your sales page on Amazon represents you and your book well. Take advantage of good keywords that will draw readers to your page. Follow my advice in Chapter Eleven about getting a professional picture made and putting your best foot forward at introducing yourself to the world. Read my chapter on keywords in my previous book (Chapter Seven), *How to Write and Publish Books*.

- Create a book launch strategy that includes getting book reviews and developing a street team. Write out a bulleted or step-by-step plan you intend to follow to launch your next book. Make sure this plan includes prelaunch, launch, and post-launch strategies (Chapters Seventeen and Eighteen).

I suggest you consider these six essentials and create your own marketing strategy. Write it out in detail and celebrate as you accomplish each step. Remember the best time to start marketing is before you've written your book, so some of the steps may need to be altered a bit as you wait on your book to come out. Nevertheless, have a written strategy (use your journal).

Bring people along for the ride. Writing can be a lonely business, so find someone in your life who shares your dream (spouse, close friend, writers' group, editor) and show them your goals. Get them to hold you accountable. Accountability does wonders for your success story.

Sign up to attend a writers' conference. It's so encouraging to meet other people just like you. You will find a network of people willing to be a part of your journey. You'll also learn helpful things at these conferences. Two of my favorite Christian conferences are the Blue Ridge Christian Writers' Conference at Ridgecrest Conference Center near Asheville, NC, and the Colorado Christian Writers' Conference in the Rocky Mountains near Estes Park. Google "writers' conferences," and you'll find a host of options.

In the Meantime...

In the meantime, write and market, write and market, and write and market some more. You'll get better by doing. Pull your calendar out now and plan your writing and marketing times for the next month. How do you want to incorporate this discipline in your life this year?

Plan your writing work and work your writing plan. That's the bottom line. Figure out what works in the area of writing and marketing and do it. Most successful writers do not wake up one morning to great success. Instead, great success comes in response to many months and years of steady, educated, and disciplined work. Stay at it, and you will be rewarded.

In the meantime, let me know how your marketing strategy is working. I'd love to hear from you. I'd enjoy celebrating your successes, and if you get stuck on something, maybe we can put our heads together and figure out how to get you moving again. You can contact me through my website: tim riordan.com.

In the meantime, write well, market consistently, and change the world.

A Word from the Author

I hope you not only enjoyed *The Next Bestseller: Book Marketing for Success* but were also inspired to put these principles into practice in your own marketing. I once heard John Maxwell say, "We are educated far above our level of obedience." I think it's also possible to be educated far above our level of application. Now that you've finished the book, you have some serious work to do. Will you first begin by stopping now to write a review of this book? I would be most grateful. Secondly, have you downloaded the "Book Launch Kit" yet? You can get that resource by visiting greentreepublishers. com/book-launch-kit.html.

I would enjoy hearing about your journey. You can contact me through my website at timriordan.com. I also write blogs about various topics related to Christian living, so feel free to join my blog list.

In writing this book, I have seen the need to focus more on a lot of topics, especially video marketing. I plan to do more research and application in this area and hope to share what I learn in a new resource sometime in the future. If you get on my email list, I'll let you know when it comes out.

I wish you the best in your writing journey.

Personal Website and Blog: timriordan.com
Facebook Author Page: facebook.com/authortimriordan
Twitter: twitter.com/tim_riordan
Goodreads.com/author/show/5538574.Tim_Riordan

Notes

Chapter Two

1. John Maxwell, Make Today Count: The secret of your success is determined by your daily agenda, Center Street—Hachette Book Group, 2004.
2. Earl Nightingale, AZ Quotes, https://www.azquotes.com/quote/526093.
3. Carole Jelen and Michael McCallister, Foreword - Jack Canfield in *Build Your Author Platform* (Dallas, TX, BenBella Books, 2014), xxvii.

Chapter Three

1. Courtney Carpenter, "The Basics of Building a Writer's Platform," http://www.writersdigest.com/writing-articles/by-writing-goal/build-a-platform-start-blogging/building-a-writers-platform, (October 22, 2012).
2. Jane Friedman, "A Definition of Author Platform," https://janefriedman.com/author-platform-definition, (July 25, 2016).
3. Brooke Warner, "Author Platform: Here's What All the Fuss is About," http://thewritelife.com/author-platform, (September 19, 2019).
4. Fiona MacDonald, "Are We Really All Connected By Just Six Degrees of Separation?" *Science Alert,* August 27, 2015, http://www.sciencealert.com/are-we-all-really-connected-by-just-six-degrees-of-separation, (August 27, 2015).

Chapter Four
1. Tim Grahl, "Your First 1000 Copies: The Step-by-Step Guide to Marketing Your Book," (Lynchburg, VA: Outthink Group, 2013), 10-11.

Chapter Five
1. Nina Amir, "6 Branding Tips for Writers and Authors," The Book Designer, https://www.thebookdesigner.com/2014/07/6-branding-tips-for-writers-and-authors/(July 16, 2014).
2. Kimberly Grabas, "Discover and Build your Author Brand," http://www.yourwriterplatform.com/build-your-author-brand, (February 23, 2013).
3. Seth Godin, "Tribes," (New York: The Penquin Group), 2008.
4. Emlyn Chand, "Discover Your Brand: A Do-It-Yourself Branding Workbook for Authors," (Union Lake, MI: Novel Publicity, 2015), digital, Loc 70.

Chapter Six
1. "8 in 10 US Adults Watch Cooking Shows," *MarketingCharts,* http://www.marketingcharts.com/television/8-in-10-us-adults-watch-cooking-shows-13719, (August 2, 2010).
2. Rick Warren, "What On Earth Am I Here For," (Grand Rapids, Michigan, Zondervan, 2012).
3. Greg Ferguson, "Audience of One," Ever Devoted Music, 1991.
4. Modo Labs Team, "Social Media Use Among College Students and Teens – What's In, What's Out and Why,"

Modo Labs, https://www.modolabs.com/blogpost/
social-media-use-among-college-students-and-teens-
whats-in-whats-out-and-why, (April 26, 2016).

5. Jack Canfield, Mark Hansen, & Les Hewitt, "The Power
of Focus," Vintage/Ebury - a Division of Random,
2001.

6. Russell Raath, "Leadership: The Power of Focus and
Thinking Differently," Forbes Magazine,
https://www.forbes.com/sites/johnkotter/2014/10/0
7/leadership-the-power-of-focus-and-of-thinking-
differently/#32a67c8379e3, (October 7, 2014).

7. Michael Hyatt, "Writing a Winning Nonfiction Book
Proposal," available at https://michaelhyatt.com/
products/ebook-writing-a-winning-book-proposal.

Chapter Seven

1. Heather Hart, "Book Marketing for Beginners: How To
Gain Confidence In Your Book Marketing And Have
Fun Doing It!" 2nd Edition, 2019.

2. Carole Jelen and Michael McCallister, *Build Your Author
Platform: A Literary Agent's Guide to Growing Your Audience
in 14 Steps* (Dallas, Texas, BenBella Books, 2014), 215.

Chapter Eight

1. Jane Friedman, "Your Author Website 101," *Writer's
Digest,* February 2015, 35.

2. Michael Hyatt, "How to Launch a Self-Hosted
WordPress Blog in 20 Minutes or Less,"
https://michaelhyatt.com/ez-wordpress-setup/

Chapter Nine

1. Guy Kawasaki and Shawn Welch, "APE: Author, Publisher, Entrepreneur – How to Publish a Book, (Nononina Press, 2013).

2. Jennifer Kane, Social Media Etiquette for Business: 100 Ways to Communicate With Grace and Class

3. Cory Janssen, *Techopedia,* http://www.techopedia.com/ definition/ 3411/platform. August 5, 2019.

4. Zephoria Digital Marketing, "Top 20 Valuable Facebook Statistics, Updated November, 2019," https://zephoria.com/top-15-valuable-facebook-statistics/

5. John Gramlich, "Ten Facts About Americans and Facebook," https://www.pewresearch.org/fact-tank/2019/05/16/facts-about-americans-and-facebook, (May 16, 2019).

6. Ibid

7. Joshua Hardwick, "Top 100 Most Visited Websites by Search Traffic (as of 2019)," https://ahrefs.com/blog/most-visited-websites, (June 25, 2019).

8. Paul Fairbrother, "The 4-Hour Work Week for Facebook Advertisers," https://adespresso.com/blog/automation-tools-facebook-ads, (January 15, 2019) .

9. Kit Smith, "52 Fascinating and Incredible YouTube Statistics," https://www.brandwatch.com/blog/you tube-stats, (July 15, 2019).

10. Christina Newberry, "130+ Social Media Statistics That Matter to Marketers in 2019," https://blog.hootsuite.

com/social-media-statistics-for-social-media-managers/#facebook, (March 5, 2019).

11. Ibid.

12. Ibid.

13. J. Clement, "Share of Online Adults in the United States Using Twitter from 2009 to 2019," https://www.statista.com/statistics/186675/share-of-us-adults-using-twitter-since-2009, (May 27, 2019).

14. Shannon Tien, "Top Twitter Demographics That Matter to Social Media Marketers," https://blog.hootsuite.com/twitter-demographics, (June 26, 2018).

15. Christina Newberry, (March 5, 2019).

16. Ibid.

Chapter Ten

1. Edie Melson, "Connections: Social Media and Networking Techniques for Writers," (Grand Marais, MN: My Book Therapy, a division of Susan May Warren Fiction, 2015).

2. Brad Smith, "15 Visual Content Marketing Statistics That'll Blow Your Mind," https://www.jeffbullas.com/visual-content-marketing-statistics.

3. Edie Melson, (2015), 31.

Chapter Eleven

1. Alex Chris, "Top 10 Search Engines in the World," Reliable-soft, https://www.reliablesoft.net/top-10-search-engines-in-the-world.

2. Greg Sterling, "Survey: Amazon Beats Google as Starting Point for Product Search," http://searchengine

land.com/survey-amazon-beats-google-starting-point-product-search-252980, (June 28, 2016).

3. Margaret Rouse, "Social Media," *TechTarget*, http://whatis.techtarget.com/definition/social-media.

Chapter Twelve

1. Sarah Bolme, "Your Guide to Marketing Christian Books, 4th ed." (Charlotte, NC: Crest Publications, 4th edition, 2019), 31.

Chapter Thirteen

1. Rob Eager, "The Author's Guide to Email Marketing," Wildfire Marketing, 148.

2. Caroline Forsey, "The Ultimate List of Email Marketing Stats for 2020," https://blog.hubspot.com/marketing/email-marketing-stats.

3. J. Clement, "Number of Email Users Worldwide from 2017 to 2023," https://www.statista.com/statistics/255080/number-of-e-mail-users-worldwide, (August 9, 2019).

4. Campaign Monitor, "Email Marketing vs. Social Media: Are You Focusing On the Wrong Channel?" https://www.campaignmonitor.com/blog/email-marketing/2019/05/email-marketing-vs-social-media, (May 21, 2019).

5. Ibid.

6. MarketingSherpa, "MarketingSherpa Survey of Consumer Attitudes towards Email Marketing Reveals Strong Preference for Email Compared with All Other Communications,"

https://www.prnewswire.com/news-releases/marketingsherpa-survey-of-consumer-attitudes-towards-email-marketing-reveals-strong-preference-for-email-compared-with-all-other-communications-300029767.html, (February 2015).

7. Nora Aufreiter, Julien Boudet, and Vivian Weng, "Why Marketers Should Keep Sending You Emails," https://www.mckinsey.com/business-functions/marketing-and-sales/our-insights/why-marketers-should-keep-sending-you-emails, (January 2014).

8. Matthew Paulson, "Email Marketing Demystified: Build a Massive Mailing List, Write Copy that Converts and Generate More Sales, 2nd Edition," (2019).

9. Brad Smith, "10 Best Email Marketing Services for Small Business," hostingfacts.com/best-email-marketing-services, (September 1, 2019).

10. CampaignMonitor, "Ultimate Email Marketing Benchmarks for 2019: By Industry and Day," https://www.campaignmonitor.com/resources/guides/email-marketing-benchmarks.

Chapter Fourteen

1. IEEE Communication Society Blog, "Cisco: Online Video to Account for 82% of all internet traffic by 2021!," https://techblog.comsoc.org/2017/06/10/cisco-increased-use-of-web-video-to-be-82-of-all-internet-traffic-by-2021, (June 10, 2017).

2. Biteable, "55 Video Marketing Statistics for 2019," https://biteable.com/blog/tips/video-marketing-statistics.

3. Ezra Fishman, "Our Videos Dramatically Increased Our Visitors' Time on Page," https://wistia.com/learn/marketing/video-time-on-page, (December 15, 2016).

4. David Hayes, "The State of Video Marketing in 2020," Hubspot, https://blog.hubspot.com/marketing/state-of-video-marketing-new-data, visited on August 22, 2019.

Chapter Fifteen

1. Scott Lorenz, "Why Authors Need a Great Headshot with Tips on How to Get One," Westwind Communications, https://www.westwindcos.com/ authors-need-great-headshot-tips-get-one.

Chapter Sixteen

1. Rob Eager, "Sell Your Book Like Wildfire," Writer's Digest Books, Cincinnati, OH, 55.

Chapter Nineteen

1. Monica Anderson, Andrew Perrin, Madhumitha Kumar, and Jingjing Jiang, "10% of Americans Don't Use the Internet: Who Are They?" https://www.pewresearch.org/fact-tank/2019/04/22/some-americans-dont-use-the-internet-who-are-they, (April 22, 2019).

Books from Greentree Publishers

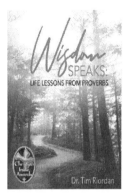

Wisdom Speaks: Life Lessons from Proverbs
By Tim Riordan

Have you ever wished for a "How To" book on life? God has given us one in the book of Proverbs. Join pastor and Bible teacher Dr. Tim Riordan on a journey through this book of wisdom where you study one of the most read books of the Bible. Through Proverbs, wisdom speaks. Are you listening? Christian Indie Award for 2019.

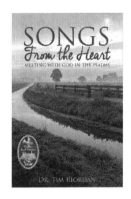

Songs from the Heart: Meeting with God in the Psalms
By Tim Riordan

Songs from the Heart: Meeting with God in the Psalms is a Bible study/ devotional on the beloved book of Psalms. Dr. Tim Riordan shares insights, Bible teaching and storytelling, making personal application to your life. Chosen as book of the year in Bible study and theology in 2016 by Christian Small Publishers Association.

Immovable: Standing Firm
In the Last Days
By Tim Riordan

Does Bible prophecy indicate we are living in the last days? What should Christians do to be ready for the days ahead? Dr. Tim Riordan shares biblical truths on Bible prophecy and how the Church can stand firm in the last days. This book also offers a small group discussion guide.

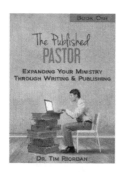

The Published Pastor: Books One & Two –
Expanding Your Ministry Through Writing and
Publishing & How to Write and Publish Books
By Tim Riordan

Would you like to expand your ministry by turning your next sermon series into a book your congregation can pass on to others? *The Published Pastor* series is a collection of books that will encourage you to write and offer you the step-by-step help you may need to become a published author.

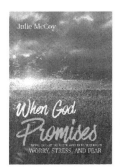

When God Promises: Taking God at His Word Will Free You from Worry, Stress, & Fear
By Julie McCoy

This six-week study draws on the experiences of people in the Bible who discovered the power of taking God at His word. As you explore their stories you will learn how trusting God's faithfulness to do what He says will give you victory over worry, stress and fear.

The Long Way Home
By Judah Knight

Dive into an adventure of scuba diving, treasure hunting, danger and suspense in Judah Knight's exciting novel, *The Long Way Home*. When Meg was stranded in the Caribbean, her life was changed through an encounter with an old friend that turned into adventure, danger, discovery, and love. Enjoy flinch-free fiction that is safe for the whole family.

Consider other books in the Davenport Series

Love Waits
By Judah Knight

Join Jon and Meg Davenport, Lacy, and Kerrick as they reunite for a treasure hunting adventure that takes them from the Bahamas on an exotic vacation that promises them more than a relaxing time away. *Love Waits* is the fifth book of the continuing story of scuba diving, treasure hunting, love, and danger. No one ever told Lacy that loving someone was so painful.

Watch for Book 6, **No Greater Love**, coming in 2021.

Ana Stillwell's Greatest Adventure
By J. W. Jenkins

Enjoy a new series written for middle-schoolers but will surely be enjoyed by all ages. Twelve-year-old Ana Stilwell uncovers a mysterious cave near her new home that leads to exciting adventures and great discoveries. Readers will encounter wonderful life principles and wholesome characters in this trilogy of books. You'll find the newly released Book Two, *Mysteries of the Mansion*, to be equally exciting, and Book Three should be released in late 2020.

For more information on any of our publications, visit www.greentreepublishers.com.

Made in the USA
Columbia, SC
16 March 2021